THE NEW
MILLENNIUM
SERIAL KILLER

To the memory Of Becky, Sian and all victims
mentioned in this work

To Jeanne, my rock, my everything.
Without you this book would not have been written –
you are the wind beneath my wings.

– Chris

To my husband Chris, and to my family,
thank you for your support in all my ventures.

– Bethan

THE NEW MILLENNIUM SERIAL KILLER

EXAMINING THE CRIMES OF
CHRISTOPHER HALLIWELL

BETHAN TRUEMAN **&** CHRIS CLARK

PEN & SWORD
TRUE CRIME

First published in Great Britain in 2022 by
PEN AND SWORD TRUE CRIME
An imprint of
Pen & Sword Books Ltd
Yorkshire – Philadelphia

ISBN 978 1 39904 098 3

A CIP catalogue record for this book is available from the British Library.

Typeset in Times New Roman 12/16 by SJmagic DESIGN SERVICES, India.
Printed and bound in the UK by CPI Group (UK) Ltd, Croydon, CR0 4YY.

Pen & Sword Books Limited incorporates the imprints of Atlas, Archaeology,
Aviation, Discovery, Family History, Fiction, History, Maritime, Military, Military
Classics, Politics, Select, Transport, True Crime, Air World, Frontline Publishing,
Leo Cooper, Remember When, Seaforth Publishing, The Praetorian Press,
Wharncliffe Local History, Wharncliffe Transport, Wharncliffe True Crime and
White Owl.

For a complete list of Pen & Sword titles please contact
PEN & SWORD BOOKS LIMITED
47 Church Street, Barnsley, South Yorkshire, S70 2AS, England
E-mail: enquiries@pen-and-sword.co.uk
Website: www.pen-and-sword.co.uk

Or
PEN AND SWORD BOOKS
1950 Lawrence Rd, Havertown, PA 19083, USA
E-mail: Uspen-and-sword@casematepublishers.com
Website: www.penandswordbooks.com

Contents

Foreword

(by Retired Detective Superintendent Steve Fulcher, formally of Wiltshire Police; the man who caught Christopher Halliwell)

Does a mother ever forget her child? What does it feel like to lose your child? How can anyone recover from the loss of a loved one? The dark nightmare of waking each morning with your child still missing can never be resolved without some hope, some knowledge, of where they are and what happened to them. At least 180,000 people go missing each year in the UK. Each of these people have countless people involved in their lives; mothers, fathers, siblings, friends, who become embroiled in a state of dark panic until they are found and returned to them. Karen Edwards describes this daily tragedy in her book *A Killer's Confession and a Mother's Fight for the Truth*.

What allows a serial killer to flourish? How does that rare cohort of people who commit the murder of strangers avoid detection? From the experience with Christopher Halliwell we can see how this can happen. He selected his victims carefully; from girls working away in the sex industry, often displaced from their home and community, thus unlikely, he believed, to be reported as missing, and if they were, the report could be to any of the 43 police forces in England and Wales other than the relevant area. Given the minimal exchange of information between these forces, no concerted effort is likely to be forthcoming to find her, certainly not within a timeframe which allows meaningful investigation to occur. Halliwell was acutely aware of forensic evidence. He was acutely aware of the need to avoid witnesses; working at night. He asked me, 'How did you catch me; was it the gamekeeper at Ramsbury?'; the only person that he identified as possibly being privy to his abduction of Sian O'Callaghan.

There is overwhelming evidence pointing to the notion that Halliwell is responsible for many further victims beyond the two murders for which he's been convicted. Not least amongst this evidence is the fact that significant number of women have come forward, to me personally, to Karen Edwards, and to the police directly, to say that they were victims of near misses at the hands of Halliwell and that, since the publicity surrounding him, they recognised him as the individual who made an attempt to coerce them into going alone with him.

When conducting the investigation, back in March 2011, I ensured that all the working girls in Swindon were contacted and accounted for. Three of those girls had had close encounters, under extremely concerning circumstances, with Halliwell who had taken them out to the Savernake Forest. He had then started behaving in such an extreme fashion; howling, pacing, threatening, that experienced working girls, became fearful for their life and phoned their protection to get them out of there.

I am one of the few people to have had a significant in-depth conversation with him. Halliwell was able to conceal his dark propensity for murder from even his close intimate relationships; with his partners and his daughters and such friends as he had. In that moment of rare contrition I could see that this was a man who had a deep predilection for cruelty and evil.

He told me that, in 2003, 2004 or 2005, he had taken a sex worker from Manchester Road in Swindon; who subsequently proved to be Becky Godden. He couldn't remember the year he murdered a woman. What that that tells me is that there are more victims. If he had only killed two women: Sian O'Callaghan and Becky Godden, it is likely, I would suggest, that he would remember which year his first victim was murdered. He told me that he buried Becky in a five-foot-deep grave. He described in some detail how he had strangled her, had sex with her and left her body at the immediate side of the wall at East Leach, a remote location in the Gloucestershire countryside. He said that he had returned the following night, stripped her of all her clothes, dug a five-foot-deep hole which took him all night. Halliwell was very specific about Becky's deposition site; he paced one foot in front of another to provide the exact spot. He had last returned to that site, he told me, some three years earlier; in somewhere around 2008. When we found Becky she was in a shallow grave. It would not be possible to dig five foot deep into the field at East Leach, because it is composed of solid clay. But in his contrite confession he was quite clear at the time. This indicates to me that there is another grave, that is five foot deep, that he confused with the one in which he had deposited Becky.

Karen Edwards, Becky's mother, commenced a campaign for 'Justice for Becky'. This involved Karen and a team of supporters campaigning across the country, collecting over 30,000 signatures on a petition for a change to the Police and Criminal Evidence Act 1984. As a consequence she received a significant quantity of information including the identification of potential witnesses who can state that Halliwell had a direct connection with Linda Razzell in Swindon and Claudia Lawrence in York; being seen physically in the company of those missing women. Karen passed this information onto Wiltshire Police on its receipt. No attempt to follow-up these potential witnesses has been made – a fact confirmed by Karen's continued contact with those parties.

And then there's the question of the sixty items of women's clothing. These were deposited at an apparent trophy store, buried in the bank of a lake in Ramsbury in Wiltshire. These items included a shot gun, folded sets of women's underwear, Sian O'Callaghan's boot and a cardigan attributed to Becky Godden. To my knowledge, no forensic work has been conducted on these items. They have not been promulgated to the next of kin of outstanding missing people across the country. Wiltshire Police specifically say that they are confident that this is a 'fly-tipping site' and that there is no evidential value in these items.

So what of Halliwell's motivation for these crimes? According to a fellow convict who shared a prison cell in 1986, Halliwell had asked, 'How many do you have to kill to be a serial killer?' and, 'Have you the ever strangled a woman during sex?' Nicholas Haggan QC, when examining Halliwell in trial in 2016 in Bristol Crown Court, drew out and demonstrated probable motive to the court; illustrating evidence of a propensity for necrophilia. Certainly, from Halliwell's own account in that trial, he murdered Sian within two minutes of her getting into his car.

The background to the case has been detailed in my book, *Catching a Serial Killer* which has been made into an ITV drama, *A Confession*. Both accounts have been limited in significant aspects due to legal constraints.

Crime investigation consists of three pillars: the gathering of witness evidence, forensic evidence and confession evidence. Witness evidence includes passive data such as CCTV and ANPR. Forensic evidence is derived from such things as murder weapons, blood-sodden clothing and the like. Confession evidence has been effectively removed from serious crime investigation by dint of the protection provided by Code C of the Police and Criminal Evidence Act 1984. When this was first incepted, I was a young detective constable. I was told by my first DI, a man of considerable gravitas, Nic Siggs of Sussex police, that these three pillars are necessary for successful crime investigations and the removal of one of the 'legs of the tripod' on which an evidential case sits, will inevitably lead to a significant collapse in the ability to investigate crime.

The Halliwell case concerns the fundamental issue as to whether a victim's Right to Life, under Article 2 of the Human Rights Act is subordinate to an offender's 'Right to Silence' under the provisions of Code C of PACE. The national Kidnap Manual, issued by ACPO

(NPCC), directs SIOs to prioritise the victim's life. Osman v UK before ECHR (1998) provides the legal precedent. However, a High Court Judge (Cox, J) and current NPCC expressed views contradict this. If NPCC have rescinded the Kidnap Manual the police service is now unclear how to act. Further, the public can have no confidence in the ability and willingness of the police to act in the interest of victims of crime. There is a lack of provision currently in PACE in exceptional circumstances such as kidnap and terrorism offences, to prioritise the Right to Life over a potential suspect's right to legal protection.

One question is this: who does the right to silence serve? How does it serve the innocent? Why would an innocent person benefit from maintaining silence when asked legitimate questions rising from suspicious circumstances which are not based on culpability? The right to silence obviously serves the guilty, because it removes that limb of evidence from the crime investigation and thus the evidential case in court. It means that the criminal must have been clumsy enough to conduct his crimes in the presence of witnesses or to have left forensic evidence behind. It protects the guilty and the earning potential of lawyers.

So there is a question as to why ACPO, (now the National Police Chiefs Counsel) defend PACE in the manner they have. PACE provides an absolution from responsibility for crime. A direct quote from a most senior officer was that 'the police are no more responsible for crime than the fire brigade is responsible for fires.' Neither notions in that statement bear any close scrutiny. The key quote from the Halliwell case was from a chief constable; 'PACE is inviolable and if the girl dies, so be it'. I was accused by the senior barrister defending Halliwell of 'single-handedly undermining the British judicial system'.

The problem the police and public are left with is this; that a police officer can have the offender in front of him, but your abducted daughter will still die and not be returned to you. My solution to this *lacuna* is to move the onus of responsibility from the police to the judiciary. PACE was introduced because of a lack of trust in police behaving properly. In Scotland and in Europe there is a mechanism by which, having formed reasonable suspicion, the party can be taken in front of an examining judge (procurator fiscal in Scotland) and the onus of responsibility passes from the police to the judiciary.

Richard Latham QC, defence counsel for Halliwell, persuaded a High Court judge that the evidence obtained from his confession was such that its probative value was outweighed by its prejudicial effect. He claimed that I oppressed Christopher Halliwell and that the prejudice he experienced was such that it outweighed the probative value of two dead bodies matched with an account as to how those two bodies came to be in a deposition site. That a judge should accept such a thing is very difficult to understand. Latham in defending Halliwell specifically undermined the value of the court and the most basic principles of British justice. He said that 'this case isn't about truth or justice it is about admissibility of evidence'. This sums up the madness that British justice has descended to. The court can listen to circumstances involving the murder of two women and remove the notions of truth and justice from their deliberations. I was driven out of the police force as a consequence. However, in 2016, a diametrically opposed judgement was delivered by a second High Court judge on the exact same set of circumstances.

Honour, duty, responsibility, truth, justice; none of these terms are in current usage. The tragedy of the case for me was that, in the heat of battle, the whole force, and surrounding forces, were all working with me with total dedication to find Sian. 10,000 people; citizens of Swindon, took time off work to search. When we found her body, on the Friday following, 10,000 Chinese lanterns were lit for her.

The police service rarely investigate anything without a specific victim complaint or an imperative forced by media attention. Throughout the intervening years, Wiltshire Police have steadfastly declined to invest resources into investigating Halliwell's crimes.

As a consequence, it is likely that those mothers, fathers, siblings and friends who have lost their loved ones, will live out their days with the sickening darkness of never knowing. Fortunately, Chris Clark, Timothy Hicks and Bethan Trueman have committed themselves and their skills to seeking the truth. Their tireless research, careful analysis and persistence has, through this book, shone a light on the potential avenues for investigation and resolution.

Steve Fulcher

16 April 2020

Introduction

Christopher Halliwell is currently in prison, serving his sentence for the murders of Becky Godden-Edwards in 2003 and Sian O'Callaghan in 2011. Despite only being convicted of these two crimes, we believe there may be evidence of his guilt in relation to a number of other murder cases that span over twenty years. Whilst he will never be released from prison and is therefore no longer a risk to society, this doesn't stop us from wanting to investigate further.

This book is a collection of the accounts of many murders and disappearances that we believe could be linked to Halliwell. There are numerous families who long for answers about what happened to the mother, daughter, sister, auntie or friend that they have lost. We have spent time investigating because we want these cases to be solved, to allow the missing women to be found and allowed a proper burial, and we long for closure and justice for their families.

Alongside these accounts, we will present to you the circumstantial evidence and other reasons that we believe suggest Christopher Halliwell is a serial killer, and why we believe that he may have been responsible for these crimes.

One of the key things that Halliwell has said which points to him being a serial killer, or at least to the idea that he was inspired by such offenders, is that whilst he was in Dartmoor Prison he asked a fellow inmate how many people you need to kill to be classed as a serial killer. The cellmate told how Halliwell was obsessed with Moors murderer Myra Hindley, saying:

> He used to ask me about killing. He said, 'How many people do you need to kill before you become a serial killer?' He just had a thing about them. He wanted people to be proud of him or an area to be afraid of him. Don't ask me why, but that's what he wanted to be. He used to get this magazine called True Detective with stories about people getting knocked off. His favourite book was about the Moors Murders with a picture of Myra Hindley on the front.

This was many years before Halliwell abducted and murdered Becky. Had Christopher Halliwell already killed by then?

During a telephone call made from prison whilst on remand in 2011, following his arrest for Sian O'Callaghan's murder, Halliwell mentioned that 'the police want to interview me about eight murders'. He was not aware that he was under surveillance at this point. The police were shocked by this because at the time they were only investigating Halliwell for the murders of the two women he had led them to, and they had not made any reference to eight such crimes.

There are a number of factors that suggest that Becky Godden-Edwards and Sian O'Callaghan are not his only victims. Before we investigate these other crimes, let's look at some more generic reasons that lead us to believe Christopher Halliwell may have killed other women.

The first thing is Christopher Halliwell's age. Whilst not impossible, it is uncommon for serial killers to begin to kill in their late thirties when they have the means and opportunity. Halliwell indeed had both the means and the opportunity to do so. When looking at known serial killers throughout the years, they statistically began to kill in their twenties; Halliwell was almost 40 when he abducted and killed

Becky Godden-Edwards in 2003. We examined convicted multiple murderers from the UK, looking at those who killed three or more people, who worked alone and were not contract killers, in the 20th and 21st centuries; there are forty-one people to look at. Of these, twenty began killing before they were 30 years old. Ten killed for the first time during their thirties, and eleven killed for the first time at the age of 40 or over. Many had a previous history of other violent crimes, therefore we think it is unlikely that Halliwell did not commit any violent crimes until 2003 when he was almost 40 years old.

In common with many violent sexual offenders, Halliwell had a fascination with hardcore pornography that he accessed online, and the searches he made even included 'child abuse' and 'bestiality'. Computer search terms he used showed he had an interest in murder, violent sex, and rape, as well as a preference for bondage. Halliwell's ex-wife told police that he would play Grand Theft Auto and get 'sexually excited when killing prostitutes in the game'. He is known to have been worried that police were investigating him over allegations involving underage girls. There has been no such inquiry into Christopher Halliwell, or allegations of this kind made, the police have said, but it clearly worried Halliwell enough for him to mention it to others.

It is very unusual for a criminal to jump from one type of crime to another in such an escalation, and that is why detectives cannot believe Halliwell committed no crimes between his burglaries and thefts in the 1980s and killing Becky Godden in 2003.

Halliwell not only went to great lengths to conceal Becky's body, but he also did such a good job of hiding her that she is unlikely to have been discovered had he not taken the police to that place. Indeed, she had been undiscovered for eight years before Halliwell led police to her remains. If this was just a moment of madness where he lashed out and lost control, as he described, we believe that it is incredibly unlikely that he would have been able to calmly dispose of her body, destroy forensic evidence and also keep the secret to himself. He even returned to the burial site over the years. Although he didn't expand on his reasonings to detectives, Halliwell admitted returning to the site on a number of occasions, with the most recent visit just three years before he killed Sian. Although he didn't expand on his reasonings to detectives, Halliwell admitted returning to the site on a number of occasions, with the most recent visit just three years before he killed Sian.

Halliwell was very forensically aware. With what has been described as a 'small library' of books on forensic science, he would have had a good knowledge of ways to hide his crimes. When he murdered Sian O'Callaghan in 2011, he removed items of her clothing and attempted to get rid of fibres that he feared would connect him to her death. He removed clothing and identifiable jewellery from the two victims we know about. Halliwell also hid the bodies in places that would be difficult to find; in the case of Becky she was not discovered until Halliwell specifically explained where she was.

Halliwell made a telling mistake when he described the depth of Becky Godden-Edward's grave. He initially told the police he had buried her 5 feet (or 1.5 metres) down, but she was found just a few inches below the surface. Police believe he may have been confused because there were other burial sites in remote areas. We believe there is a woman somewhere, buried in the deeper grave he mistakenly believed was Becky's, someone whose family have still not had their loved one returned to them for a funeral and proper burial.

In a number of the cases discussed within these pages, the victim's bodies were not found for weeks, months or even years after going missing, having been disposed of by someone who knew the best place to hide a body where it would remain undiscovered. We will also present to you cases where the body of the woman has still not been found, and we believe this points to victims suffering the same fate as Becky Godden-Edwards; women buried in final resting places that may never be found unless their killer reveals where they are located.

Another key piece of information that suggests Halliwell could be responsible for many other murders is his request to strike a deal with police, which was that if he cleared up Becky's murder, the police would never interview him about anything ever again. Of course, this deal could have been made because he simply didn't like talking to the police, or that there were other petty crimes in his past, but we believe it points to other secrets he doesn't want revealed.

The transitory nature of Halliwell's job history is also key. In common with serial killers such as Peter Sutcliffe, who was a lorry driver, Robert Black, who was a delivery van driver, and Levi Bellfield, who worked as a bouncer and security guard, Halliwell's job as a taxi driver gave him the opportunity to abduct and murder. A car featuring taxi markings provides the perfect cover for driving around the streets, especially at night, and offers a false sense of comfort to prospective victims.

As well as this, Halliwell held an interest in narrowboating and love of such holidays meant he could travel all around the country recreationally. The use of a narrowboat meant he had an additional mode of transport, away from crime scenes, that others wouldn't have available to them, and that the police may not think to check. A boat could also be harder for police to trace.

The Kennet and Avon Canal is local to where Halliwell lived in the years prior to the murders of Becky and Sian. Many of the places it runs past or through will be named in this book as areas where women went missing or were killed.

The Kennet and Avon Canal is an impressive feat of engineering, made up of two river navigations and a linking stretch of canal. It runs from the Severn Estuary near Bristol to the River Thames at Reading, it is over 100 miles long with more than 100 locks, features some magnificent engineering and flows through some of the most beautiful scenery in southern England. It was reopened in 1990 after decades of dereliction.

The Avon Navigation cuts through wooded hills and the famous Avon Gorge on its way to Bristol before it meanders up to Bath. The canal then climbs the Caen flight of locks to Devizes and runs amidst rolling hillsides along the Vale of Pewsey towards Hungerford to descend through pasturelands, woods, and water meadows to Reading and the junction with the River Thames.

The distance between Sian's deposition site and a pond at Ramsbury where Halliwell liked to fish is seventeen miles. Extensive searches of this pond in the Hilldrop Lane area were carried out after detectives learned that this was an area Halliwell visited frequently. They began their searches in 2016, when they learned of the spot, using a specialist dive team from Avon and Somerset and cadaver dogs from South Wales. Officers spent hours draining and sieving thousands of litres of water from the 8 foot deep pond, performing a fingertip search of the area. They found sixty items in total in the pond and buried in the surrounding area. These items included a cardigan that had belonged to Becky Godden-Edwards and boots belonging to Sian. They were the boots she had been wearing the night Halliwell took her, that police had been searching for since her murder. Serial killers are known for taking trophies, so it is reasonable to believe that a number of, if not all of the other fifty eight items belong to women who were sadly also victims of Halliwell's over the years.

The FBI have stated that when repeat offenders keep an item from their victim they generally do this for one of two reasons. They have either taken a souvenir, an item used to fuel a fantasy, or they have taken a trophy, which is proof of their skill. This allows a killer to feel powerful, according to *The A to Z Encyclopaedia of Serial Killers* by Harold Schecter, a leading authority on serial killers, and David Everitt. Nicole Mott, the author of *Encyclopaedia of Murder and Violent Crime* further clarified that the trophy is used to preserve the memory of the victims to aid in sexual acts, and becomes a signature, a part of a killers murder ritual. When Halliwell's home was searched, items that did not belong to members of his household were found, items such as a perfume bottle. Were these also trophies?

In his book, Steve Fulcher said it is 'scandalous' that it has taken Wiltshire Police so long to acknowledge what he believes has been clear for some time. He argued the discovery of clothing and other items pointed to a murderer hoarding 'trophies' from previous victims. He said: 'If my suspicions are right, if the evidence in the trophy store suggests a truth that still lies hidden, then Halliwell had a prolific propensity to murder – perhaps as often and once or twice a year.'

We agree.

We will be presenting to you cases where descriptions of suspects match Halliwell, and where vehicles are described by witnesses, that match vehicles available to Halliwell or potentially were at his disposal. We will discuss how Halliwell was a strong, fit man, who was also referred to as a 'ladies man', easily able to charm the women he met, and that he has links to all the areas discussed.

The women whose cases we will discuss were all vulnerable in some way at the time of their murder or disappearance, due to a number of factors, and we believe Halliwell took advantage of this.

We are not the only ones to hold such suspicions. In June 2017 a report in *This Is Wiltshire* described the potential that Christopher Halliwell may have murdered dozens more women; explaining in the article that this was a conclusion reached by Steve Fulcher in his book, *Catching A Serial Killer*, and is a theory that Wiltshire Police has only recently been willing to acknowledge. Speaking after the 2016 trial, Detective Superintendent Sean Memory, who took over the investigation from Steve Fulcher, said: 'Halliwell talked candidly in 1985 about wanting to be a serial killer and I genuinely believe that's a distinct possibility.' In April 2020, retired detective Mike Rees pledged that if he was elected as the next Wiltshire police and crime commissioner, he would launch a new investigation into Halliwell. Although unsuccessful in his election campaign, the media focussed on his pledges and the idea of further investigations into Halliwell's potential other crimes. Becky Godden-Edwards' mother Karen was vocal also in the media about her support of this.

Steve Fulcher has accused Wiltshire Police of being reluctant to explore the full extent of Halliwell's potential offending, even going so far as to say they had declined to interview witnesses whose details were passed to them. He stated: 'One witness came forward to say they were sure they had seen Halliwell and still-missing Claudia Lawrence together. Given the description of a man connected with Claudia's case is identical to Halliwell and she went missing on the same day of the year as Sian – March 19 – you might think that witness statement would be taken, but it never has been to my knowledge.' Claudia's mother, Joan Lawrence, asked police to let her look through the clothing found at Ramsbury in a bid to potentially identify items belonging to her daughter. It has not been confirmed whether or not she was given this opportunity.

In a challenge to his former employers at Wiltshire Police, Steve Fulcher wrote: 'Whoever the six – or sixty – other victims are, they are real people with mothers, fathers, siblings and friends. People's lives have been wrecked, for the rest of time, by whatever has happened to their relative. A police investigation that fails to scrutinise every possible clue is one that fails families. It fails victims.' Steve Fulcher has also stated 'If this is his trophy store the potential victims that you highlight could be linked by the obvious expedient of showing the clothing to their Next of Kin and making potential DNA comparisons.' We agree, and believe it is in the public's best interest that Wiltshire Police make descriptions or photographs of the items found here public.

This book catalogues a series of unsolved murders and reports of missing women from between 1988 and 2011 which we believe match up to the elements of Halliwell's two murder convictions. Some cases with convictions which have similarities are also discussed. Are those convicted for these crimes actually innocent and serving a sentence for something Christopher Halliwell was actually responsible for?

We have also considered cases which appear to have links with various canals and waterways throughout England, proposing that Halliwell's recreational interest in narrowboat holidays provided him with the means and opportunity to strike, as well as an option for his getaway that may not have been suspected by police. We researched them in chronological order following Halliwell's release from prison in 1987 and wherever there are clear clusters of crimes, we have chosen to present these in chapters together.

We believe there are a number of ways the police could look into other crimes for which Halliwell could be responsible. Oddly, considering he was himself a murderer, albeit not one the police were aware of, Halliwell was a serial complainer to the police and other authorities. Between 2000 and 2010 he made numerous reports about perceived slights and wrongs against him. These could help build up the timeline of Halliwell's whereabouts if the police were to investigate the cases we have included in this book in more detail.

In correspondence with Steve Fulcher in June 2017, we described the cases we believe fit with Halliwell's profile as a potential serial killer, and the former detective superintendent agreed the *modus operandi* details were consistent with the facts attributable to Halliwell. He confirmed that in 2011 he and his team had undertaken extensive intelligence and antecedence research, which included eighty vehicles registered to Halliwell. This research included makes, models and dates of ownership. His employment and housing history was also recorded. Naturally whilst Steve Fulcher has no access to this any longer, the police would still have this information available to them.

As part of the investigation into Halliwell prior to the trial for Sian's murder, his ex-wife Lisa handed over his work diaries from the years 2000 to 2005 (although unfortunately for police the diaries from 2001 are missing). Officers may be able to map his movements in some detail for what may be a crucial four-year period, alongside the large number of vehicles registered to his name over the years potentially linking him to other murders or disappearances where witnesses have described specific cars.

There were a number of sketches recovered from Halliwell's home during Wiltshire Police's searches following Sian's murder.

The sketches showed areas of natural beauty, sketched by Halliwell, and some have suggested that these could well point to deposition sites of other victims. These twelve sketches have not been released to the public, despite author Chris' continued Freedom of Information Requests.

The police also have at their disposal the DNA sample Halliwell provided which tied him to evidence in Sian's case. In a number of the cases we will present throughout this book, DNA samples were taken, and whilst of course these would not have been compared to Halliwell's at the time, we suggest this is a simple way to rule him out of such investigations should the police wish to do this now.

We feel sad that it feels to us like there has been a lack of transparency from the police over the years, and we find it really hard to understand the unwillingness from the police to engage with the public on this topic. We can't see why detectives are so unwilling to look into these unsolved crimes. Indeed, we believe that they should instead welcome the opportunity to look into these crimes further.

What do they have to lose? Is it down to a fear of being shown to be incompetent, with mistakes made during initial investigations? Perhaps, but often we see stellar police work being done and still no leads. If they do feel the initial investigation wasn't up to standard, why not make amends? Perhaps the police forces feel unable to look at all avenues due to a lack of funding and resources, but we would argue they could take advantage of the public providing them with information and suggestions.

Whatever the reason, we would like them to investigate further. Whilst Halliwell is incarcerated for life and is no longer a threat to society, these women and their families have still not received any answers or closure, nor the justice they deserve.

Chapter 1

Christopher Halliwell

The Making of a Serial Killer

Christopher Halliwell was born Christopher John Halliwell in Swindon, Wiltshire, in early 1964 to parents Alan Halliwell and Zofia Hanns; the pair were married in April 1963 in Huddersfield. In 1965, Halliwell's sister Sarah was born.

It is hard to find out much about Halliwell's childhood, but from our research it does not sound like he was a happy child. When Zofia separated from Alan, she took the two children to Scotland where they settled in Galloway with her new husband. Here Halliwell was subjected to physical and mental abuse at the hands of the people who should have loved him unconditionally. Halliwell was beaten when he misbehaved and he and his sister are said to have been regularly hit with a leather strap and were even dragged out of bed in the middle of the night by their mother and her partner who ruled with 'cruel discipline'. Understandably, he grew to hate his mother, and as a result of this difficult home life, Halliwell grew to be what people have described as cold and emotionless.

The majority of violent killers have suffered some form of abuse in their formative years, taking the pain they experienced and turning it onto others in an attempt to feel powerful instead of the victim. It is also often the case that they have issues around relationships relating to their mother. As we will go on to explain, it has been suggested that the reason Halliwell murdered Sian O'Callaghan was because she reminded him of his own abusive mother, who he ended up despising.

1

It is easy for us to see Christopher Halliwell as a monster and a killer now we know so much about the horrific crimes for which he has been convicted, but at the time that his crimes were revealed it was a shock to many who knew him. After all, this was a family man with plenty of friends and acquaintances, whose job meant he was well known locally. However, for Halliwell's sister Sarah, this was not such a shock. She had known that her brother had a dark side since childhood and that he displayed what she has described as a 'disturbing aura'. In an interview in 2011, when Sarah had not spoken to her brother in over two years, she said:

> He was just not a normal child. I have witnessed things he did at first hand, and it was very unpleasant. He loved trapping spiders and butterflies and taking his time to pull off their legs and wings one by one. It was like a hobby to him, and he showed no emotion while he was doing it. He has always lived in a strange world of his own.

Sarah described Halliwell's chilling blue eyes, saying: 'He is a very cold, detached person who could never handle normal relationships. If you ever had a go at him, he would just stare you out with those vile eyes and say nothing.'

Sarah described her brother as 'an evil, manipulative bastard' who she thought would 'believe he had won' after getting away with Becky's murder and she added:

> He's done at least two murders and probably many more. He's playing games with the law and the families of the victims. He should be strung up or shot. He will always be dangerous because he is a completely cold fish. He doesn't relate to people or care about them at all. I never want to see him or hear his name again. As a mum myself its Sian's parents I'm thinking of.

2

Halliwell is remembered as being a quiet boy and an unusual character by his classmates from Dalbeattie, a town in the county of Kirkcudbrightshire in Dumfries and Galloway, Scotland, where he spent his teenage years. A former schoolmate of his has described him, saying: 'We remember a quiet, thin and rather strange boy. The family came here for a few years and then left just as suddenly. It's all a bit odd when you look back. Chris was certainly a very strange individual.'

Halliwell lived in Dalbeattie in the late 1970s and early 1980s, attending the local high school before working for a few months in Carson's butchers where he became skilled at knife work. Workmate Norman Neilson said: 'This quiet, thin young boy arrived one day. He was about sixteen. He did the sweeping up and cleaning as well as very basic butchering tasks, such as paring bones and helping make pies and sausages.' But Halliwell, despite having this job, was looking for other ways to make money. He did so in a dishonest fashion, a move that was perhaps his first foray into criminal behaviour. Neilson continued: 'A few months later, his mum came into the shop looking for him and telling us she had to take him to the bank to apologise. She said he'd been filling in imaginary sums of cash in his passbook then trying to withdraw the amounts.'

When Halliwell was 15 years old, his mother decided she could no longer cope with looking after her son and chose to put him into foster care. Halliwell showed virtually no emotion when she did this, simply telling her that he hated her and that he would get her back for it. Zofia died in 2009, and Halliwell's family later told the police that he had developed a 'deep, lasting hatred of her' and that he would react in an extreme manner if he saw a photo of her, smashing doors and ripping up furniture before laying sobbing. Halliwell was close, however, to his father Alan, an RAF worker, who died in 1992, and he spent time visiting him over the years.

After leaving school, Halliwell moved to Swindon. In his spare time he discovered a love of fishing, became a keen angler and developed an encyclopaedic knowledge of waterways and ponds. He had various jobs over the years, drifting from one form of employment to another, including working as a window cleaner, as well as in the building trade and in construction. He liked to drive and at different times in his life he worked as a chauffeur and a taxi driver. He also had illegal means of getting what he wanted. In his early years he would steal cars, and he also utilised his job as a chauffeur to study the layout of upmarket country houses which he later burgled. He was sentenced to four years for these burglaries in the mid-1980s, of which he served less than three years at Dartmoor Prison in Devon.

Christopher Halliwell was released from HMP Dartmoor in 1987 when he was aged 23 years old. In the early nineties he married Lisa Byrne, a shop assistant, and they lived in the Broad Green area of Swindon where they raised their three children. Lisa later described Halliwell saying he was 'a loner' with few friends when they met. They were together for fifteen years until she discovered that he had cheated on her. Neighbours recalled a strained marriage, with one person who had lived near to the couple later commenting: 'They were living together but they weren't getting on well. There were problems between husband and wife.' Halliwell left Lisa before moving in with his new partner Heather Widdowson who lived a few doors down the road.

He lived with Heather until his conviction for Sian's murder, keeping his secret life completely separate to his home life, although she knew he'd had troubles in the past. She said later:

> He was quiet and normally kept his feelings to himself but he once told me he'd done 'horrendous' things when he was young but I didn't want to know what. I knew he'd been in prison and had a difficult childhood. He was beaten by his mum from the age of three and left home at 16. But now I know he's a sick man.' After learning about his crimes, Heather said, 'I've no feelings for Chris now. He is a cold, callous coward and I'll never forgive him for what he has done.

Halliwell started as a taxi driver, before working his way up and starting his own chauffeur business. This didn't work out, and in January 2010 he was declared bankrupt, and so he returned to working for private hire cab companies. By this time he had become a sociable man; he had a number of friends and acquaintances, and enjoyed a drink. We spoke to a local man who had been a friend of Christopher Halliwell's for years, and he told us that Halliwell's go-to drinks were lager or blended whiskey. Halliwell also liked to listen to music and his favourite genre was described by this former pal as 'heavy music'. Ex-wife Lisa described him as a moderate drinker and said that he regularly smoked cannabis before going to bed.

Halliwell lived in Swindon for a long time, and in his capacity as a night-time taxi driver he got to know the local red light district well through driving sex workers and drug dealers around. By his own admission, Halliwell often paid sex workers for their services, and was unfaithful to his partners, enjoying numerous one-night stands. He told the police, 'Occasionally, I would use a call girl. They work in a certain area around Swindon.'

The red light district described in this book refers to certain areas of Swindon: Manchester Road, Broadgreen and Station Road. The original red light district area of Swindon was around Station Road, but according to the *Swindon Advertiser*, when the layout of the road changed in 1981, a number of the sex workers moved to Manchester Road. The police estimated that in October 2008 there were forty-two on-street sex workers in the area, but in more recent times they have estimated only a few remain. This area was popular as a red light district due mainly to its locality; it is an area close to the train station and bus station as well as being in the heart of the town.

A lot has been done to try to take sex workers off the streets. Residents formed a street watch group, hoping to change the area in which they lived. In the late 2000s Operation Dobbin was launched by police which aimed to take sex workers away from the streets and offer them treatment for addictions to hard drugs if required. There is also a local trust that works alongside the police called the Nelson Trust. The Nelson Trust's Sex Worker Outreach Project (SWOP) offers practical and emotional support to women involved in street-based sex working across Wiltshire, offering food, clothes, condoms and a friendly face to these vulnerable women. They also offer practical support and safety advice as well as access to women's centres, where they can receive a range of specialist interventions. However, despite the work done by the local residents and councillors, volunteers and police, the area continues to maintain this reputation for sex workers working on the streets.

People who knew Halliwell have said that he had a reputation for being a womanizer, a bit of a ladies' man. One taxi driver, who used to work with Halliwell, said at the time: 'He works the late shifts and is a regular on the nightclub runs. He's slim and has piercing blue eyes and I suppose women would find him quite attractive.' Once the details of his crimes were made public, people would say they had previously had bad feelings about Halliwell, but his partner Heather later said to the press: 'We had a happy, loving relationship. In all the time we were together he never showed any anger towards me. It never crossed my mind that he was capable of hurting me.'

Halliwell is currently being held at HMP Long Lartin prison, a Category A men's prison located in the village of South Littleton, near Evesham in Worcestershire. Here high-profile inmates like Halliwell are treated as 'vulnerable prisoners' – or VPs – and held on a protection wing. These wings house sex offenders, child killers, former police officers, former prison guards and prisoners who have testified against other people. Essentially, these are people who would be vulnerable to attack if put amongst the general population in prison.

A source described how, in these wings, prisoners are let out for around twenty to thirty minutes in the morning for a shower and to move around. They are given five minutes to get their lunch at about 12.30pm and then take their food back to their cells to eat. The inmates are also given forty-five minutes exercise time should they wish to use it at 2pm, with dinner served at 4.30pm, and sometimes the inmates are given communal time known as 'association' where they can chat and watch television and socialise.

Christopher Halliwell is still often the subject of media interest, and news articles give us a glimpse into his life behind bars. In 2016 a report in the *Swindon Advertiser* stated he was earning £17 a week for tobacco and coffee, and that he had written back to some of his following of autograph hunters. According to letters penned from his prison cell, he has come to terms with the fact that as a heterosexual man he will never have another sexual partner.

But in general, the articles printed are not much more than gossip; in 2017 it was reported that, according to officers, Halliwell has become a practising Satanist, worshiping the Devil. Whilst some of the other inmates were apparently scared of this, others simply remarked that he had probably just 'watched *The Omen* too many times'.

One consistent theme with news reports and articles in the media is that Halliwell revels in his notoriety, boasts he is the most famous killer in the prison system, and is regarded as one of the most dangerous men locked up at Her Majesty's pleasure today.

Chapter 2

Sian O'Callaghan

Sian O'Callaghan was 22 years old when she went missing on 19 March 2011. A bright, bubbly young woman with many friends and a loving family and boyfriend, Sian's disappearance sent shockwaves through her hometown of Swindon. In the days that followed, the widespread press coverage meant her case was discussed both locally and much further afield.

Described as a happy girl, Sian was close with her family; her mum Elaine told the press that she was a doting sister, and like a second mother to her youngest brother. Sian had tried college after her GCSEs, but her mum said that it just wasn't for her, so she got a job in administration. This was something she really enjoyed. In March 2011, she lived with her boyfriend Kevin Reape at a flat that the pair had moved to that January, in the Old Town area of Swindon.

Known for its bars and shops, Old Town is seen by many as the heart of Swindon, with numerous community events and a busy nightlife. It has a rich and varied architecture, is home to the picturesque Lawn Woods and Town Gardens, and is just a few minutes' walk from the main town centre and the shopping precinct, the Outlet Village.

In the early hours of 19 March, Sian left a popular local nightclub called Suju, after a night out with friends, to walk the 800 metres home. The evening out had been a rare treat for Sian, who was saving up for a New York trip with Kevin. She was caught on CCTV leaving the club at 2.52am.

Sian had texted Kevin asking, 'where are you?' at 1.24am, but she didn't respond to his reply at 3.24am, 'in bed, you?' When she did not return home, Kevin was understandably worried. He phoned around family and friends, as well as the hospital, but was unable to find his girlfriend. After hours of worrying, hoping she would walk through the door any minute, at 9.45am the next day Kevin contacted the police to file a missing persons report.

Sian's older brother had phoned their mum, Elaine, who was away for a weekend in Warwickshire that morning. She said that at the time she '…thought it was a bit of an overreaction and that she'd probably just crashed at a friend's house.' But when Sian still hadn't reappeared by lunchtime, she began to get concerned. Elaine arrived home that afternoon to police officers at the house. They were asking about Sian's normal behaviours and she later said it suddenly felt like things had escalated really quickly.

Kevin volunteered to go to the Swindon police station to help with enquiries and willingly surrendered his mobile phone and the key to the flat he shared with Sian. The police also checked his phone, his Facebook account and his computer, and swiftly eliminated him from any suspicion for the disappearance of Sian.

On 20 March, the police issued a public appeal for information and revealed to the media that they were searching the 4,500-acre Savernake Forest thanks to information discovered using mobile phone cell site analysis. They were able to determine that the time that had elapsed between Sian's appearance on the club's CCTV and her mobile phone pings at 2.52am and 3.24am meant that the journey from Swindon to the forest could only have been made in a vehicle.

Leading the investigation for Wiltshire Police was Detective Superintendent Steve Fulcher, and on 21 March Sian's boyfriend and family joined him to appeal for information at a news conference. During this, Detective Superintendent Steve Fulcher said to the press:

> Sian left Suju and walked along the High Street in Old Town and there were a number of vehicles moving through the High Street between 2.55am to 3am. We would like to identify the people in those vehicles as possible witnesses. I'd also like to hear from anyone who saw any vehicles in or near beauty spots between Swindon and Savernake between 3am and 4am. It is very important that people come forward as they may have vital information which will help us to find Sian.

Half an hour's drive from the town centre of Swindon, Savernake Forest is Britain's only privately owned forest, a 4,500-acre forest situated between Marlborough and Great Bedwyn in Wiltshire. It is popular for picnics, walkers and is a registered important historic park, rich in history.

On 22nd March, a real sense of community was felt as social media was utilised and approximately 400 locals rushed to help with the police searches, everyone hoping and praying that Sian would be found alive. Online and in the press, women were warned not to walk alone at night and to be vigilant to any danger. An anonymous donor offered a £20,000 reward for information that would lead to finding the missing young woman. This reward was doubled shortly afterwards, such was the urgency felt in the search to find Sian. In this small, tight-knit community, her disappearance was such a shock; you just don't believe things like this can happen so close to home. Residents displayed police appeal posters asking for information in their vehicles, and shop keepers displayed them in their windows.

The police worked fast, reporting that they were 'very close' to identifying Sian's whereabouts, bringing in specialist dog teams and examining what they described as 'hotspots' in Savernake Forest.

After discovering CCTV showing that a police vehicle with ANPR on board was passing at a significant moment, the police had identified a dark-coloured car with what looked to be taxi markings on it that had been seen between Swindon and Savernake Forest shortly after Sian had disappeared.

ANPR, or Automatic Number-Plate Recognition, uses optical character recognition on images to read vehicle registration plates to create location data about vehicles. Here in the UK, there is a network of nearly 8,000 cameras capturing between 25 and 30 million ANPR records daily, which are stored for up to two years in the National ANPR Data Centre. UK law enforcement agencies can access these records to use as evidence in their investigations.

This lucky break gave them a hit on a Toyota Avensis which was owned and driven by a local taxi driver, Christopher Halliwell. Working under the assumption he had taken Sian and was keeping her somewhere, they decided to follow him and place him under round the clock surveillance rather than immediately arrest him, in the hope he would lead them to Sian.

On the night that Sian had disappeared, Halliwell had signed off from work but, instead of going home, he had cruised the streets of Swindon looking for a victim. The police spoke to the taxi firm Halliwell worked for, who used a GPS tracking system with messaging and call recording facilities. The firm provided the police with the information that Halliwell had taken his last fare at 1.10am on 20 March, phoned in to say he was going home at 1.58am, and then switched his system off at 2.13am on 20 March. It remained off until 6.53pm that evening. But the police could see that Halliwell had not headed home after work at all, rather that, for about forty minutes, he had been driving around the town centre and Old Town areas of Swindon.

Detectives believed Halliwell had spotted Sian during his drive around the area and had chosen her as a potential victim, before luring her into his car under the pretence of being a legitimate lift home. CCTV showed that the street was empty as Sian made her way along the road away from the nightclub. Sian's boyfriend Kevin had often suggested she shouldn't walk home, that even if she was somewhere as close to their home as the nightclub Suju, she should instead take a taxi. When a taxi driver stopped beside her, as she left the club intoxicated, she most likely felt she was following this good advice and doing the right thing. However, instead of driving towards her home, Sian would have very quickly been terrified to realise that the taxi was heading in entirely the wrong direction, and out of Swindon. Later Halliwell would admit that he had killed Sian 'within minutes' of leaving Swindon. He claimed that Sian had asked him to drive her to a part of Swindon called Covingham, trying to explain away the reason for driving in the wrong direction, but this was easily disproved by looking at the roads used and direction in which the taxi travelled.

Whilst under police surveillance, on 22 March, Halliwell was observed cleaning the rear seat of his taxi with cleaning fluid and then putting seat and headrest covers in an industrial wheelie bin. The following day, he made further efforts to get rid of evidence by burning more car seat covers by the roadside. The police were sure that his actions were in an effort to remove any evidence that could link him to Sian's murder and, in fact, the seat and headrest covers he discarded were ultimately found to have Sian's blood upon them; the police confiscated these immediately on observing his behaviour and sent them for forensic testing.

Halliwell was also seen driving around and out of Swindon, leading Steve Fulcher to believe that he was holding Sian against her will, somewhere around Barbury Castle, an Iron Age hill fort nearby on the Ridgeway route. A fifteen-minute drive from Swindon town centre, Barbury Castle is a beautiful site with a view across to the Cotswolds and the River Severn, and it is a popular walking route. It is remote; other than a couple of nearby farms, there are no homes near the site, and it is only accessible via a single road, making it a popular walking route as well as popular with horse riders.

On 24 March, after surveillance showed Halliwell buying an overdose-quantity of painkillers, Detective Superintendent Steve Fulcher ordered his team to make their move in case their main suspect planned to take his own life. Halliwell was arrested on suspicion of kidnap in the car park of a local Asda supermarket, where experienced detectives carried out what they called an 'urgent interview' with Halliwell. This meant they arrested him and asked him questions at the scene, rather than taking him to Gablecross Police Station. Halliwell told them he didn't know the whereabouts of Sian and requested to speak to a solicitor.

When he was stopped by the police, Christopher Halliwell was actually displaying one of the 'Help Find Sian' posters in the back of his car. This has been seen by many locals as an act of contempt, although of course this could well have been part of his plan to ensure no one suspected he was involved. It had also been reported that Halliwell had told a passenger that morning that he was a friend of the family of Sian O'Callaghan, mates with her dad, and that he had made comments about the kidnapper saying, 'If I found the bugger, I'd kill him'.

As previously discussed, the 47-year-old taxi driver was well known in the Swindon area and, at the time of his arrest, lived in a suburban semi with his partner Heather Widdowson and her three daughters. As news leaked out about the suspect, people who lived nearby were shocked, telling the press that he seemed like a nice guy who would always have a smile on his face. One fellow minicab driver said to the press: 'Real nice bloke, a genuine bloke, a normal run-of-the-mill bloke. I've got two daughters I would have trusted them in his car.'

After arresting him in the car park of the supermarket, Fulcher made the decision to take Halliwell to Barbury Castle, where he believed Sian was being held, instead of to Gablecross Police Station in Swindon. He chose to do this for two main reasons; primarily because he believed that immediate further questioning was the best way to protect Sian's life if she was still alive, but also because Fulcher believed there was a place in investigations for the policeman's 'gut instinct' and he wanted to look Halliwell in the eye and speak to him at the place he believed Sian was being kept. Halliwell was taken in a patrol car driven by a police officer, with Steve Fulcher and his scribe Deborah Peach. Deb, as she was known, was a civilian employee of Wiltshire Police, the PA of Steve Fulcher's boss, and in her role as a scribe she was expected to follow Steve Fulcher around, recording his every move and conversation for the investigation's record book.

For the next four hours the team of police officers waited anxiously as Steve Fulcher and Halliwell sat out in the open, smoked cigarettes and spoke; Fulcher chipping away at Halliwell's refusals to open up, asking him to tell them where Sian was. His persistence eventually worked, when finally Halliwell asked him, 'Got a car? We'll go'.

Steve Fulcher already knew that his informal chat with Halliwell could be challenged under Code C of the Police and Criminal Evidence Act (PACE)*, which protects the rights of an individual against the police with regard to questioning and detention, and his actions could be seen to be contravening these rules. Halliwell had already been cautioned twice, but according to the procedure, Steve Fulcher should have done it again, and he should have repeated to Halliwell that he had the right to speak to a solicitor. But Halliwell hadn't specifically stated he had killed Sian, he simply asked Fulcher if he had a car, and Fulcher didn't want to lose this valuable opportunity, so he made the decision not to caution Halliwell again. He said later: 'It's a simple moral issue, I did these things because they were the right things to do in these circumstances. In fact, they were the only things to do.'

Halliwell, sat in the back of a patrol car, directed the police to drive out of Barbury Castle and the four of them headed out of Swindon on the A420. Above the car, a police helicopter followed their route, while behind the car snaked a line of patrol cars in a convoy. Halliwell

---

For more detail on PACE guidelines, please refer to Appendix Two.

led the driver to a tiny road near Uffington, and they made their way past a farm to the place where Halliwell had left Sian's body; a remote stretch of road with grass verges. He was able to point them to a section to search, before he was returned to the patrol car. It was here, down an embankment, that the police found Sian.

Sian's body was found lying face down and was naked from her waist to her ankles. She was partially concealed amongst the undergrowth and had been positioned down a steep bank where she would not immediately be seen by a passing motorist.

A Home Office pathologist carried out a post-mortem examination and found that Sian had died from the combined effects of two stab wounds to the head and neck, as well as compression to the neck. There was further evidence of blunt trauma to the back of the head and areas of external deep bruising to her face. The head trauma, including a skull fracture, could have been caused by her falling, being pushed to the ground or by her head being forcibly struck by a broad object. The post-mortem confirmed that the bruising on her body was consistent with being punched or kicked, and the bruising to the neck could have been caused by either compression, blunt force trauma or a combination of both. Halliwell had removed her underwear and leggings and sections appeared to have been cut from the crotch area of those garments. Her bra had also been removed. During a news conference on 26 March, Detective Superintendent Fulcher stated that tests had revealed that Sian had not been sexually assaulted.

Sian was similar visually to Halliwell's mother, who, as we discussed earlier, he hated for the abuse she had subjected him to, and some have suggested this was one of the reasons he chose Sian when he was driving around looking for his victim that night.

The police charged Halliwell with Sian's murder on 26 March, after she had been formally identified by her mother's partner. The police discovered that in the twenty-four hours after he had abducted Sian, Halliwell had made four visits to the place in Savernake Forest where he had hidden her body. Halliwell admitted to carrying out a reconnaissance for a possible deposition site. He had left Sian's body in the forest, but when he realised police were searching there, he knew he had to make a change. By the early hours of the 21st, Halliwell had moved Sian's body from Savernake Forest to the spot where it was later found. Not only had he carried her a distance, but he had been able to lift her body over a wall, which shows the strength this man had. There had been a short time during the surveillance where the team had lost Halliwell; frustratingly for detectives it transpired that this was when he moved Sian.

Luckily for the police, Halliwell's attempts at a clean-up were not entirely successful. And although he had burned items of clothing and taken the time to get rid of seat covers and floor mats from his car, the forensic examinations found Sian's blood in the rear of the car.

As the investigation progressed, the police learned more key information. Halliwell, it transpired, was the father of one of Sian's friends, and in the days after her disappearance, Halliwell told a colleague: 'Who knows what or who you find buried out there, there could be loads of people over the years.' A police source later explained:

> There is the chilling thought that Sian was not the first and Halliwell may have been roughly working to some dreadful blueprint from previous incidents. Sian was picked up in the early hours of the morning outside a club in Swindon. Sian, of course, did the right thing and got into a cab to take her home, a cab driven by the father of one of her friends at that.
>
> Halliwell has then driven her out of Swindon in his green Toyota Avensis and away from her home. This was obviously under duress, probably under threat from a shotgun.

The source said the cabbie would have driven along the A346 to Marlborough and along the A4 into the Savernake Forest, adding:

> We know from her mobile phone records that Sian was in the Savernake half an hour after she was picked up by Halliwell. What we now know is Halliwell must have then taken her out of the forest, across the A4, on to a narrow lane that winds down to join the road from Marlborough to Ramsbury. He probably took a left turn on to the Aldbourne road and then right on to Hilldrop Lane at the next junction. She may have died at Hilldrop but she was buried miles away at Uffington, on the other side of Swindon in the Vale of the White Horse. Hilldrop Lane is not an obvious spot, not even to a cabbie, and it's fair to surmise Halliwell had been there before. If it turns out the items of clothing found at Hilldrop belong to more than one missing woman it would go towards confirming the rather chilling theory that he may have had a routine.

This apparently respectable family man had a much darker side, and detectives discovered that Halliwell was regularly using sex workers and that he had, in recent weeks, got 'rough and weird' with them. Some of these women had been so frightened they had felt the need to call for help. As people began to reflect on their own experiences with Christopher Halliwell, their eyes opened to a different man to the one they thought they knew.

One local woman we spoke to said:

> I knew Halliwell when I was a teenager, he lived next door to a school friend in Ashbury avenue when he was still married to Lisa. We often used to chat to him and his daughters and they seemed like a nice family. He had on a couple of occasions offered me lift home I politely

declined. Sometime during winter 2002/03 which we now know was around the time of Becky Godden's murder. I was stood outside with a few friends with myself facing towards the road, I saw Christopher leaving for night shift it was dark. He reversed out of the drive and suddenly stopped looked right at me and although only for seconds it felt like minutes, his eyes were black and his stare was very intimidating. I can't describe it but I've never seen anyone look like this before or since. I immediately thought he's up to something maybe an affair or criminal activities but never murder. Every now and then I thought about that stare even before Sian's murder. I now believe that I had seen his mask slip so to speak.

Another person we spoke to told us of his disgust at realising that this was the man his parents had trusted enough to babysit him, saying:

I knew his kids since they were toddlers, and my mum and dad would be out drinking with them often. He would often babysit for me and my sister, as my parents did the same in return with his kids if he needed them to. It's grim now to realise what he was really like, but no one had seen that side to him.

Living just a few doors away from Halliwell at the time of Sian's disappearance, his neighbour told us of the shock she felt when she heard about his crime:

It wasn't unusual for me to stumble home in the early hours of the morning after a night out, filled with that youthful ignorance of danger, drunk and happy following a night out. The shock we felt as a family when we learned what had happened really changed things. My mum would tell me and my friends that no matter the time, if we were unable to get a lift home, we were to ring her and she would come and pick us up.

As well as this revelation being shocking to people who knew Halliwell, people who lived in the area were also astonished to discover that such events had occurred so close to home. We spoke to a local woman who told us:

I live with my family about 200 metres from Suju nightclub. When you see true crime documentaries and read books about it, you often hear that old cliche, 'You'd never expect it to happen here.' It is so true in this case, though! Old Town, the part of Swindon in which it happened, is a bustling and lively part of the town. There seem to be people there; always. It has a livelier night life than the town centre. I love living here, but the reason I point out how busy it is here, even early in the morning, is that it shows to what extent Christopher Halliwell went to get what he wanted and that is really scary. I now have a young son and I walk and or drive past both venues almost every day. Totally honestly, I think about Sian and Becky. I sometimes get goosebumps walking where Sian would have been picked up and think how quickly and easily it happened. He was a 'professional.' He knew exactly what he was doing and I think it was down to having had lots of practise. This kind of person seemed so far away from this place that I love, but he really wasn't. I also live opposite road that Sian lived in. She was so close to getting home and to safety. Swindon has most definitely changed since this happened. I still see artwork dedicated to Sian on walls in quieter parts of the town. It touched everyone.

On 28 March 2011, Halliwell was remanded in custody by Swindon magistrates to appear before Bristol Crown Court on the 30 March, and at this point, no application for bail was made. Halliwell was remanded to appear via video link at Bristol Crown Court on 8 April. Sian's inquest was opened and adjourned on 1 April.

In the week that followed the discovery of Sian, hundreds of people marched through Swindon in an event organised to support Sian's family, to pay respects, and to show that the area was still a safe place to live. The march began at Suju nightclub, was led through Old Town by local priest Father Mark Paris and culminated with prayers and a minute's silence in a nearby park at the Lawn. There was also a vigil held at the Polo Ground, where hundreds of Chinese lanterns and balloons were launched into the night sky and a two-minute silence was held as part of the 'Lighting Up The Sky for Sian' gathering.

On 18 April, Sian's funeral was held and whilst it was a private funeral, hundreds of people lined the streets to pay their respects as the cortege drove slowly past, with a police escort. It felt like the whole town had come to a standstill.

When the murder case came to court, Sian's mum Elaine made sure she sat in the seat closest to Halliwell, facing him, explaining that the reason for her position was to show her strength, 'I wasn't going to let him intimidate me. We made eye contact a few times, but he always ended up looking away.' On 31 May 2012, Halliwell appeared in court at a plea and case management hearing and pleaded not guilty to the charge of murdering Sian O'Callaghan. Perhaps he thought he could get away with this plea but the evidence was stacking up against him. A swab taken from an injury to Sian's left breast had revealed a mixed DNA profile with components from Halliwell, showing him to be a possible contributor. In addition, there was the blood in Halliwell's car, and police also had CCTV footage and automatic number place recognition (ANPR) evidence to put him in the Old Town area when she had been taken. A forensic odontologist had inspected the injury to Sian's breast and concluded that biting might have caused the bruising, but Halliwell refused to supply a dental impression. The police had also recovered the items from inside Halliwell's taxi that he had attempted to clean and burn, linking these to Sian through DNA.

Thankfully, that October, Sian's family were told Halliwell had changed his mind and would plead guilty, sparing the family a trial. On 19 October 2012, Halliwell officially pleaded guilty to the sexually motivated murder of the 22-year-old, at Bristol Crown Court. He was sentenced to life imprisonment with a minimum tariff of twenty-five years, with the judge commenting on the number of aggravating factors in the case. These aggravating factors included Halliwell abusing his power in his position as a taxi driver, the premeditation of the attack, the vulnerability of the victim and the extensive efforts he made to conceal her body. The judge, Mrs Justice Cox, did concede that the guilty verdict spared Sian's family a trial, and so she reduced the suggested sentence of thirty years to twenty-five. Halliwell was told that if he was released, he would be placed on licence for the remainder of his life. The sentence was upheld in the appeal court later that same year on 14 December.

The police and prosecution have described the murder as sexually motivated as, whilst Sian was not sexually assaulted during the attack, Halliwell's actions were sexual in nature. In sentencing, Mrs Justice Cox said:

> I am satisfied on the evidence, viewed cumulatively, that this was a murder involving sexual conduct. I reject the submission by your counsel that I cannot be sure of that on the evidence in this case. The Prosecution do not suggest that there is, here, any evidence of overt sexual activity. Sexual conduct can, however, take many forms and again I view the evidence cumulatively.
>
> Her injuries included injuries to her left breast and nipple consistent with bites or another form of aggressive assault. Her body was found half naked, with her leggings

and underwear around her ankles. These factors, together with the cutting away of fabric from those items of clothing in the crotch area and the removal of her bra, point clearly to sexual conduct. Had Sian survived, this evidence would have amounted to evidence of a sexual assault.

After the sentencing, a statement from Kevin was read out in court, in which he said: 'Words cannot describe the pain and anguish I felt during these six days she was missing. My heart was ripped out, my life has been destroyed. Sian was a beautiful, happy-go-lucky person who could cheer up the most miserable of people. I will spend the rest of my life being grateful for the time we had together.'

The police had worked hard to identify and arrest Halliwell, and they were so pleased to finally have a conviction, and that they had managed to secure justice for Sian and her loved ones. But there was more to the story; Halliwell hadn't just taken them to Sian's body.

After he had indicated the section of road the police needed to search for Sian, Christopher Halliwell had informed Steve Fulcher that he wanted to speak to him more. Steve Fulcher interpreted Halliwell saying 'you and I should have a chat' as him wanting to strike a deal with the police, perhaps in relation to his family who would naturally be affected by the revelations. Steve Fulcher, Deb, the scribe, and the driver of the patrol car, headed up to the nearby White Horse, again with Halliwell in the back of the car. The White Horse is a tourist site just outside Swindon, and this remote setting provided Steve Fulcher with the opportunity to sit and speak one on one with Halliwell again. When they arrived, the four got out and once again Steve Fulcher provided Halliwell with a cigarette, and waited to hear what Halliwell had wanted to talk about. The pair began to speak.

Steve Fulcher was shocked when, out of the blue, Halliwell asked 'Do you want another one?', and told him that he had killed someone else, and that he could take them to where she was buried also.

Again, Steve Fulcher chose not to return to Gablecross Police Station, not because he was hoping to find the missing young woman alive this time, but because he didn't know whether Halliwell would tell him anything further in such a formal setting. With no information about the name of the victim or even the place she was buried, Steve Fulcher needed Halliwell to cooperate. Halliwell directed the driver of the patrol car on another journey, this time leading the police convoy on a twenty-mile car journey to Eastleach in south Gloucestershire before taking the police on foot to a point in a remote field called Oxo Bottom.

It was here that the police later made the sad discovery of the headless remains of Becky Godden-Edwards, who Halliwell had killed and buried eight years previously.

Chapter 3

Becky Godden-Edwards

When Detective Superintendent Steve Fulcher was interviewing Halliwell in his search for Sian O'Callaghan, he was clinging onto the hopes that he would find the 22-year-old alive. This time, with Halliwell leading him to another body, Steve Fulcher had no such expectations. In stark contrast, he was hoping with every second that passed that Halliwell wouldn't suddenly change his mind about taking them to this other woman's remains. He therefore chose once again not to return to the formal setting of Gablecross Police Station, and made the decision not to caution Halliwell, not wanting to break this spell, this rapport they seemed to have developed.

After leading the police on a forty-five minute drive to Oxo Bottom, a nondescript field in Eastleach, Gloucestershire, the police began their search for the second body. This run-of-the-mill farmer's field would soon reveal its grisly secret.

Whilst he wasn't able to be specific about the dates or even narrow down the year, Halliwell said he had taken the young woman that they were going to find from the Swindon area at some point between 2003 and 2005. He also told them that he had 'had sex with her and then strangled her.'

He told the officers he was a 'sick fucker' and at one point asked Steve Fulcher 'Is it too late to get help?'. He also said: 'I know you aren't a psychologist but what the fuck's wrong? Normal people don't go round killing.' He explained how he had killed this victim by strangulation and that he had then taken off all of her clothes before leaving her hidden in bushes. Halliwell explained that he had returned the following evening to bury her, spending the night digging a grave. He also told them that he had returned to the site over the years.

The headless skeletal remains were recovered, and the police began to investigate just who this woman was, whilst continuing to be frustrated with Halliwell's refusal to explain what he had done with the woman's head. This is not something he has ever answered and remains a mystery to this day; detectives even ordered for Halliwell's conservatory to be excavated in case the skull was buried there, and questioned Halliwell on its whereabouts, but to no avail.

Amongst the tips called in by friends and families of missing women, the press could only release that 'the remains are thought to be those of a woman aged in her mid to late 20s.' Speculation was rife. Names of women who had been missing for years, including Claudia Lawrence, who had gone missing two years to the day before Sian was murdered, and Sally Ann John, a sex worker who had gone missing in Swindon in 1995, were discussed amongst others.

But eventually the police announced that the remains had been identified as the body of Rebecca Godden-Edwards, who had been missing for eight years. The police had matched the DNA of the remains to personal items provided by her family. Steve Fulcher broke the news that her body had been found to her devastated family on 4 April 2011, what would have been Becky's 29th birthday.

Becky's childhood was by all accounts a happy one, growing up in a loving family alongside her brother, but her teenage years had been difficult; blighted with self-harm, solvent abuse and rebellious behaviour that escalated in a short period of time. In her book *A Killer's Confession: How I Brought My Daughter's Murderer to Justice,* Becky's mum, Karen Edwards, describes her daughter as vulnerable and troubled and explains how this change came about following nasty bullying at senior school.

Karen writes about how Becky had been at senior school for just weeks when she had dog mess smeared on her by a group of girls, and how the bullying was relentless. When she was just 11 years old, Becky attempted to take her own life by ingesting a large number of medicines including paracetamol, ibuprofen, antihistamines and sleeping pills, and whilst she had some good days at school, she continued to suffer at the hands of bullies. By the age of 15 the family decided it would be better for Becky to be home-schooled and she saw a tutor. This worked well; Becky was happy again, and she did well at her schoolwork. It seemed that a corner had been turned, and eventually Becky returned to mainstream education at a new school for her exams.

It appeared at first that Becky was doing well at her new school. She attended regularly and took pride in her schoolwork and homework, but a series of events began to lead Becky down a dark path. The catalyst, according to Karen, was that Becky's dad had a new baby with his partner. From this point on the rebellious behaviour really began, with Becky staying out late, being cheeky, and having mood swings. Karen eventually discovered her daughter had been using inhalants and when she confronted Becky about this, Becky ran away from home to stay with a friend.

Soon, Becky's behaviour escalated, and sadly so did her drug taking. Karen discovered her daughter was 'chasing the dragon', inhaling the vapours from heated heroin. This time when she confronted her daughter however, Becky asked her to help. Here began a cycle of the family doing their best to support Becky through rehabilitation and getting healthy, before she was dragged back to a life of drug abuse by the lure of her friends.

After a few years, Becky had turned to sex work to fund her habits, often disappearing for weeks or months at a time before returning home to her desperate mum and family who wished they could help her out of the cycle. Karen last saw her daughter in 2002, after picking Becky up from the magistrates court. She was meant to go home to stay with her mum but on the drive back, she had asked her mum to stop at her boyfriend's house. Upon leaving the car, Becky told her mum that she would come home when she was ready. Whilst Karen knew that her daughter would take drugs again in the house, and pleaded with her to come home, she also knew that if she forced the matter Becky would simply run away. So, Karen drove home and waited, holding on to hope for her daughter's safe return, as the months turned to years.

In a sad and cruel twist, Karen had been told by many friends and loved ones that they had seen Becky whilst she was considered missing. She had held on to the hope of finding her daughter, appealing on missing persons websites and driving around Swindon at night praying she would catch a glimpse of her. Every time she was told by friends and family about sightings of Becky, Karen's resolve that she would one day be reunited with her daughter was strengthened, and she made sure to buy and wrap birthday and Christmas presents for Becky, leaving these in her bedroom for her to open on her return. There were two new gifts on the top of the pile, wrapped and waiting, on the day the police arrived with the news that her daughter had been found.

It became apparent that Halliwell had been a regular client of Becky's when she worked as a sex worker in Swindon. Another local sex worker told the court at his trial that Halliwell was 'a bit besotted' with 20-year-old Becky, and that he had sometimes given her money so she did not have to work. Becky was officially last seen around January 2003 getting into a taxi outside a local nightclub, Destiny and Desire, although due to her troubled life and the rumoured sightings, she was not reported missing officially by her family until 2007.

Halliwell had taken advantage of Becky's vulnerability as a drug addict and sex worker. On the night she was last seen, she had been standing outside the nightclub with a friend when Halliwell turned up in his taxi and summoned her. He was well known for driving drug dealers and sex workers around the local area. Becky was clearly not interested, and returned to join her friend but Halliwell remained, and a row developed which culminated in Becky eventually getting into the back of the taxi, described by her friend as being 'annoyed and huffed.' The following day, Halliwell went to his GP and was treated for a broken little finger and scratches to his face. It would be fair to assume that these injuries were sustained during Halliwell's attack on Becky, but as her remains were skeletal when they were eventually recovered, it was impossible to ascertain whether she suffered defensive injuries at the time of the attack.

Killers tend to have a 'type', and this can be seen here with Halliwell's choices of victims. Both Sian and Becky were slim, petite and attractive. Both had vanished from Swindon town centre and were last seen leaving nightclubs. Whilst they had been in totally different lines of work, some believe Halliwell may have mistaken Sian for a sex worker. This is because when he was asked whether he knew Sian was not a sex worker by police, his response was 'I do now'.

The bodies of both women were disposed of in rural locations over the Wiltshire Police boundary in two separate border counties. As well as attempting to destroy forensic evidence by disposing of, cleaning, and even burning items from his taxi following Sian's murder, detectives believed the reason Halliwell had removed Becky's clothing prior to disposing of her body was also to ensure there were no links between her and his taxi, or to himself. Halliwell admitted to the murders of both young women whilst taking Steve Fulcher to their deposition sites, but once back at the police station he changed his story, claiming he wasn't responsible. He refused to answer any questions posed to him from that point on, and simply stated that he was innocent.

Whilst incredibly frustrating, this did vindicate Steve Fulcher's actions. We are sure that had he not spent the time he did with Halliwell building some form of rapport, Becky's murder and final resting place would remain a mystery to this day.

Even though Halliwell had taken the police to Becky's body, and said he had abducted and killed her, at the pre-trial hearing the judge, Justice Laura Cox, made a decision that meant Becky's case wouldn't go to court.

Because of the way Steve Fulcher had garnered the confession from Halliwell about Becky's murder, Justice Cox ruled that the evidence gleaned from the interview – Halliwell's confessions to killing each of the women as well as the fact that Halliwell had taken police to the bodies – could not be used in court. This was due to the fact that Detective Superintendent Steve Fulcher had breached the guidelines of the Police and Criminal Evidence Act 1984 by failing to caution Halliwell and denying him access to a solicitor during the period that the confessions were obtained. This meant there was not enough evidence to bring a case against Halliwell for Becky's death, but as there was other evidence relating to Sian, her case could proceed. Therefore, the charge that he murdered Becky in Swindon, on a day between 27 December 2002, and 1 January 2006, was withdrawn.

In his book, Steve Fulcher describes in detail his reasoning for not cautioning Halliwell, citing his decision to instead use the guidance given to police in their kidnap manual. He said: 'I had only minutes to make the decision. Was I going to do this? Was I going to breach PACE in order to save a girl's life? It was literally a do-or-die scenario.'

Steve Fulcher later mentions the internal struggle he felt about not cautioning Halliwell again once he said he would take him to the site of Becky's body. Halliwell was offering to take him to the site of another murder victim but, until they got there, they didn't have a name or any information to go on, and Halliwell wasn't even sure of the year he had killed the woman in question. Steve Fulcher writes: 'I felt I couldn't stop until he had led me to the deposition site. More important than PACE compliance or any future evidential presentation in court had to be the recovery of the body: because until "another one" became a dead girl with a name and a face and a family, we didn't have a case at all.'

In September 2013, the Independent Police Complaints Commission published the results of their investigation into Steve Fulcher's actions. They found that Steve Fulcher had a case to answer for gross misconduct for breaches of the Police and Criminal Evidence

Act and for ignoring force orders. In January 2014, the IPCC described Steve Fulcher's actions as 'catastrophic', and he was found guilty of gross misconduct. Although still employed by the police, after being given a final written warning by a disciplinary tribunal, Fulcher took leave from work and began taking antidepressants and sleeping pills. Until this point, he had never been professionally reprimanded in his career, he had only ever received commendations; three crown court recommendations and one chief constable's commendation. He received strong backing about his actions from the families of Sian and Becky, with Becky's mother stating 'Had he have followed the guidelines, then Becky would never have been found, she would never have come into the equation'. Karen even launched a petition to have PACE changed to offer greater protection for police officers like Steve, but it was not enough for him. Having worked in the police force since the age of 21, ascending through the ranks from constable to detective superintendent, the toll this took on Steve Fulcher was shown by his resignation from Wiltshire Police in May 2014.

Over the next four years, detectives worked to gather evidence linking Halliwell to Becky's murder, in the hopes that they could convict him without using his confession. When police searched a remote pond in Hilldrop Lane, Ramsbury, where Halliwell liked to fish, they found Sian's boots. These were the boots that she had been wearing the night he abducted her, that were missing when she was found. They also discovered dozens of scraps of material and clothing; in total their efforts unearthed around sixty items of women's clothing and accessories. One such item was a knitted cardigan that was determined to have belonged to Becky. The police painstakingly mapped Becky's last movements and matched them to where Halliwell was at the time. They also showed that soil found on tools in Halliwell's shed was probably from the field where Becky's remains were found.

On 23 April 2013, an inquest at Oxford Coroner's Court into the death of Becky Godden recorded a narrative verdict stating that the cause of her death, believed to have been in 2003, was 'unascertained but probably caused unlawfully by a third party.' Such a cold and unfeeling way to describe the final moments of this young woman's life, and phrasing that, to us, diminishes the impact her murder had. That she had been hidden so effectively, along with the fact that her head was never found shows that she definitely was killed by a third party, rather than 'probably'.

Finally, in 2016, the Crown Prosecution Service challenged the ruling that the evidence against Halliwell obtained after his arrest was inadmissible because Fulcher had breached PACE. This new pre-trial hearing was heard by His Honour Sir John Griffith Williams, who overturned Mrs Justice Cox's ruling and allowed all of the evidence obtained by Steve Fulcher to be heard.

On 31 March 2016, Halliwell was charged with the murder of Becky Godden before magistrates in Chippenham. On 2 April 2016, Halliwell pleaded not guilty to Becky's murder and the trial began at Bristol Crown Court on 5 September 2016, a trial in which Halliwell represented himself. Frustratingly his not guilty plea this time meant that unlike with the first court case, the family of his victim had to sit through a full trial describing what had happened to their loved one. In a touching gesture Sian's mum and boyfriend also attended the trial.

In an attempt to hide the true reason why he knew where to find Becky's remains, Halliwell told the jury he was given £700 by two drug dealers to drive them to that remote area, insinuating that these unknown men were the real killers. Endeavouring to display his honest nature, Halliwell admitted that he had killed Sian. He attempted to portray himself as a reasonable man, someone who had simply lashed out at Sian when she drunkenly attacked him, but instead of proving to the jury what a good guy he was, the admission opened Halliwell up for a line of questioning about his actions surrounding Sian's murder. It was through this questioning that damning information was uncovered. Not only had Halliwell killed Sian within minutes of picking her up but he had returned four times to interfere with her body, to remove items of clothing, and to move her to a new deposition site.

During his questioning about Becky's murder, however, Halliwell continued to state he had nothing to do with the crime, denying everything and repeating the story he had made up about the drug dealers. He refused to admit that the crime had been sexually motivated, even though the evidence suggested that it had been, and he had admitted to having sex with Becky prior to her murder. He tried to convince the jury that the only reason he had admitted to Steve Fulcher that he had killed Becky in the first place is because it was all part of an elaborate plot to ruin his career in the police. Luckily, all of this was easily seen through, and after less than three hours of deliberation, the jury found Halliwell guilty of Becky's murder on 19 September 2016. Halliwell reportedly smirked and laughed when the guilty verdict was returned.

On 23 September, Halliwell was sentenced to life imprisonment with a whole life order, meaning he will never be eligible for parole. In his sentencing remarks, Sir John Griffith Williams said of the murder: 'I conclude you must have attacked Rebecca Godden; that attack must have been prompted by her refusing you sex. When she put up a struggle, you killed her. You clearly intended to kill her. I add that I am certain she struggled desperately in an attempt to save her life but she was physically no match for you.' He described how he felt like Halliwell had contradicted himself when he said he had wanted to spare Sian's family further grief, explaining that if he hadn't wanted to cause them further grief he wouldn't have made 'no comment' answers when interviewed about her murder, and he had done this once again to Becky's family, both with the 'no comment' answers and not pleading guilty.

Discussing the defence Halliwell had put forward, Sir John Griffith Williams said: 'After what must have been hours of trawling through the prosecution papers, you devised a cock and bull story about two drug dealers.' He described Halliwell, saying: 'I have had the opportunity of observing you throughout the trial and listening to your evidence. I have no doubt that you are a self-centred and domineering individual who wants his own way. You are both calculating and devious.'

Outside court, Becky's mother, Karen Edwards, said: 'It has been an extremely painful journey but today we have received the justice that has felt like an eternity for our beautiful little girl Becky. We have all sat and listened to heart-breaking evidence day after day.'

She also spoke about Steve Fulcher, thanking him for finding out what had happened to her daughter, saying: 'I would like to thank him from the bottom of my heart for bringing my little girl home. I will always respect him and be indebted to him for making that moral decision as a police officer.'

So, if these two murders were the only crimes he was guilty of, why would Halliwell, when being questioned by detectives for the second time about Becky's murder, say to the police: 'I don't want to keep coming back every couple of years on different charges. If I can clear this up in the next few hours, will everything else be forgotten?'

We believe that this points to other secrets Halliwell was concealing and that the clues to potential other crimes are hidden within his 'trophy stash': who else did the clothing and other items recovered from the lake belong to? When Halliwell first instructed the police to dig at Oxo Bottom, he made an error about the depth of Becky's grave, and the police believe he may have been confused because there were other burial sites. It is also statistically unlikely that Halliwell wouldn't have committed any attacks between these two dates in 2003 and 2011; the idea that a sexually motivated murderer would have such a large gap in the time frame between his only two murders is unusual when looking at patterns of serial offenders.

Chapter 4

Claudia Lawrence

The disappearance of 35-year-old chef, Claudia Lawrence, shocked the nation in 2009; her story has been the subject of much discussion over the years and has gripped the public, who continue to speculate on what happened to her. She is yet to be found. Claudia's was one of the names put forward as a potential identity for the body found at Eastleach, before police identified her as Becky.

Born in the market town of Malton, North Yorkshire, Claudia had what her father described as a happy and contented childhood with her parents and an older sister with whom she was very close. She loved all things equestrian, and from a young age until the summer prior to when she went missing, Claudia had her own pony or horse. Whilst her sister wasn't as interested in this hobby as Claudia, she still got involved. The sisters would spend a lot of time together in their teens going for rides on the weekends and enjoying each other's company together around the stable yard.

At the time of her disappearance, Claudia was living in Heworth Road, York, and working one mile from home at The Lounge, a student restaurant at the University of York's Goodricke College in the Roger Kirk Centre. She was a talented and creative chef, but also had a head for business, helping with the other side of running a kitchen and effectively taking the role of catering manager at times throughout her career.

Claudia was really satisfied with the house she had bought. She enjoyed decorating and furnishing it, and took pride in the fact that her job as a chef allowed her to pay her mortgage and run a car herself. She enjoyed holidays with friends and had an active social life, although if she was booked for shifts this took precedence as work was important to this responsible young woman. Even when she wasn't with friends, like most young people she would be chatting with them, texting or calling. She kept in touch with her family regularly too.

The area she lived in, Heworth, is no longer specifically called a village but according to residents it has a small town feel. Claudia, by all accounts, was well known and would stop to chat if she saw people she knew in the street. She was a regular at her local pub, the Nag's Head, which was close to her home.

On 18 March 2009, Claudia went to work as normal; however because her car was in a garage for repairs she had to walk to the Lounge instead. Whilst unusual, it wasn't the first time she had made the half an hour walk. Getting to work on foot had meant she had to leave quite early – estimated at around 5.30am – and she was caught on CCTV arriving at the university at 5.57am. Luckily when work finished that afternoon and Claudia headed out at just after 2.30pm, she was able to get a lift home with a work colleague instead. The pair chatted together on the drive back to Claudia's house. She changed out of her chef whites into a white t-shirt, blue jeans, and trainers and popped back out. After posting a letter and stopping to talk to a woman at roughly 3.05pm, Claudia went home where it's thought she remained for the rest of the day.

That evening, Claudia spoke to her dad on the phone at about 7.30pm. Later, at just after 8pm, Claudia spoke to her mum on the phone when they made plans to spend Mother's Day together. Claudia's mum later recalled that the pair had both been watching the same television show in their respective homes. Claudia spent time texting with friends until a final text was sent from her phone at 8.23pm and since that time, Claudia has not been heard from again. A text message sent to her at 9.12pm from a friend who was a bar worker in Cyprus was not answered but, due to her phone not being a smartphone, it isn't known whether she read it or not. The time she went missing wasn't obvious for police, she may have already come to harm by this point, or she may just have gone to bed.

Claudia was due at work the next day at 6am, another shift that she planned to walk to. But Claudia didn't turn up, which was unlike her. She had made plans to see her friend at the pub that evening, and when she didn't arrive or reply to her friend's messages and calls, her friend became increasingly worried. This friend asked the landlord of the Nag's Head if he had seen her, and he actually walked the four doors down from the pub to Claudia's house on the morning of the 20th to try and get an answer from her. There was no answer. The friend then called the local hospital, but again drew a blank. She contacted Claudia's dad Peter who called the university, and at this point he realised Claudia hadn't made it to work on the 19th. He drove over to Heworth, concerned about what he might find, and apprehensively let himself into Claudia's home, but there was no sign of her. It looked to her worried dad that she had got up for work, left the house, but had not arrived at the Lounge, or returned to her home.

By this point, Peter was beside himself with worry, knowing this was unlike his daughter, and so, later the same day, he anxiously reported Claudia missing to North Yorkshire Police. The police were unable to find a reason for Claudia to want to vanish, and because it was so out of character for her to disappear, North Yorkshire Police worked on the assumption that she had been abducted. From the beginning they treated her disappearance as a crime, not a case of someone voluntarily going missing.

Claudia's passport and bank cards were where she usually kept them. She had her own house and a job she wouldn't usually not turn up to; this was not some teenage runaway scenario. There was no immediately obvious reason for her wanting to leave and she had no plans to go away anywhere that were known to her family or friends. Colleagues who were later questioned as part of the investigation into

Claudia's disappearance would say that nothing appeared out of the ordinary when they last saw her and Claudia was her usual self .

The police appeals generated a number of witness statements describing unusual behaviours spotted around the time of Claudia's disappearance.

A man wearing dark-coloured clothing and carrying a rucksack had been seen on CCTV loitering near to the back gate of Claudia's home on the evening of the 18th, the last day she had definitely been seen alive. The CCTV footage showed him walking towards her back garden, disappearing out of the camera's range for approximately one minute, and then walking back towards the main road. It appeared that as he turned the corner, he spotted another man in the street and suddenly stopped, as though he was attempting not to be noticed. Investigations showed the man from the evening of the 18th had been acting in the suspicious manner again on the morning of 19 March, walking down the alley at 5.07am, disappearing for roughly a minute and then back into range again. This was ultimately a dead end however, when North Yorkshire Police identified him as a man who owned a number of properties in the area who was simply checking on the homes, and he was eliminated from their enquiries.

A man and a woman were seen standing on the route Claudia would have taken to work, facing each other several feet apart on Melrosegate Bridge, on the morning of the 19th at around the time Claudia would have been walking to work. The man was described to be wearing a dark hooded top, with a skinny build and a receding hairline, and he was smoking from a cigarette held in his left hand. The woman matched Claudia's description and the witness said she was wearing a blue jacket, which is what Claudia would have been wearing.

There was another witness who described seeing a man and a woman, although without any physical descriptions, talking in what looked like an agitated manner, perhaps arguing, on the embankment up from the road Claudia would have walked along to get to work, and that a car was close by with the door open.

The police determined that Claudia's mobile phone was deliberately turned off by someone at about 12.10pm GMT on Thursday, 19 March 2009. Of course, it is not known by whom, or whether the battery just ran out, so it might not have been deliberately turned off, but the data suggests that if it was turned off, Claudia was not the one to do it as she should have been at work for 4 hours at this point.

Claudia's blue and grey Karrimor rucksack in which she carried her chef's whites has never been found. In a statement issued by North Yorkshire Police on their website, they appealed for information about a rucksack that had been spotted. They confirmed in their appeal that Claudia's rucksack was missing, and a similar one had been spotted near the University of York at about 1pm on Thursday, 19 March 2009. The location of this rucksack was in a grassy area off a footpath which runs between Heslington Road and Walmgate Stray, which is just past The Retreat if you were heading towards the university, and the police were keen to know whose it was. The land around the area was subsequently searched, but as well as not finding the rucksack, they found no clues either, so it was important to them to know whether this was connected to Claudia's disappearance.

A DNA profile of a male was established from a cigarette butt found in Claudia's car, which was being repaired at the time she disappeared. It wasn't unusual for Claudia to allow people to smoke in her car or her home, but police wanted to identify the man it belonged to. We suggest this profile should be compared to the Halliwell's DNA sample on file. Perhaps the police already have compared these; if this has been done the findings should be released to the public.

Six weeks after Claudia went missing, the investigation into her disappearance was formally reclassified by North Yorkshire Police from a missing person's case to a suspected murder enquiry, even though there was no physical evidence found that a crime had taken place or that she was dead.

In Claudia's house, officers found an empty blonde hair dye box and rubber gloves, but it isn't known whether Claudia had been adding highlights to, or dying, her own hair, or a friend's. The bed had been made and there were what appeared to be breakfast dishes in the kitchen sink. Claudia's electric toothbrush was also left on the kitchen draining board. These details all support the theory that she left for work on the morning of Thursday, 19 March 2009.

The investigation was hampered by the fact that Claudia didn't have a smartphone at the time she went missing, and she also didn't have any social media profiles. The police were able to track her phone, but this simply showed them that the phone did not leave the area before it left the phone network when it was turned off.

Of particular interest to the investigation team was that Claudia's hair straighteners were missing from her home. In their appeals to the press, the police said:

> From the review of all the evidence available, including the fact that Claudia's bed was made, and it appears that she had eaten breakfast and brushed her teeth, it is our belief that she had left for work on the morning of Thursday 19 March 2009. What is unusual is that Claudia's GHD hair straighteners – model number 14.4.1B and purchased in May 2007 – were missing from her home. It appears that Claudia used highlights in her naturally brown hair. In relation to Claudia's hair straighteners, helpful information was passed to the investigation team which established that she may, on some occasions, have taken them to work. The GHD hair straighteners remain outstanding and the appeal to find them still stands.

In May 2009, a website was launched to appeal for information about Claudia's disappearance. Newspaper and television appeals continued, and more missing posters were displayed. In June that year, a reconstruction of Claudia's last known movements was featured in a BBC Crimewatch appeal, and the independent crime-fighting charity

Crimestoppers offered a reward of £10,000 to anyone providing information which led to the arrest and conviction of any person linked to the disappearance. The BBC Crimewatch appeal also featured a reconstruction of the couple seen arguing along Claudia's route to work. Also that summer, Claudia's dad Peter Lawrence launched a YouTube appeal for information, but there were still no leads.

In October 2009, North Yorkshire Police revealed they were looking for the driver of a 'rusty white van' who had been seen trying to talk to women on Claudia's route to work in the days before Claudia disappeared. The van was outside the fish and chip shop for at least 30 minutes from 9.01pm on Wednesday, 18 March 2009, as confirmed by CCTV footage on a passing bus.

Sadly, there were aspects to the investigation that hindered North Yorkshire Police, for example, the fact that the photo of Claudia which was used initially in appeals for witnesses showed her with an old hair style, which may have meant potential witnesses didn't realise they had seen the missing 35-year-old at the time. The official photo appeared to show her with a lighter-coloured style, but her usual stylist at a local salon told police he had coloured her hair using a darker dye than normal, just three-and-a-half weeks before she disappeared.

The distance of Claudia's walk to work was incorrectly reported as 3 miles when it is actually 1.3 miles. As part of our research, Chris visited York and physically walked the route Claudia would have taken to work, confirming that the walk would take about 26 minutes.

We were not particularly impressed by North Yorkshire Police's investigation into this 'rusty white van', the white Vauxhall Astra van sought by police for elimination. In just five minutes research on Google we were able to identify the vehicle and the property it was registered to. We used three photographs to highlight the information we found and passed this information on to the North Yorkshire Police Control Room. The first photo showed a white Vauxhall Astra van which was captured by CCTV from a bus turning into Heworth Road at 9pm on Wednesday, 18 March 2009; this was the photo shown on the BBC Crimewatch appeal during 2014. The second image was the police appeal superimposed with Heworth Place and, in this image, we highlighted a vehicle we had found via Google Street View. The final image is of either the same, or a replacement, van parked at the end of Heworth Place within 50 yards of Claudia's address. This image was captured September 2014. We were able to establish who the owner vehicle, and the previous one on CCTV, were at this time.

On the fifth anniversary of Claudia's disappearance, a new appeal was made on the BBC's Crimewatch, which aired on 19 March 2014. More CCTV footage, recovered in 2009, showed a silver Ford Focus hatchback car driving along Claudia's street and that the brake lights had lit up as it approached Claudia's home. But again, despite this appeal, no more leads were forthcoming, and Claudia Lawrence's disappearance remains unsolved.

So why do we believe Christopher Halliwell could be responsible for the murder of Claudia Lawrence?

It is known that serial killers prefer to operate in areas they are familiar with and know their way around. Therefore, when we are looking at other crimes potentially committed by Halliwell, it is necessary to identify areas we know that he was familiar with. . In September 2016 the *Daily Mail* reported that Halliwell's father had lived in Huddersfield and, it has also been reported, in the York area, possibly in the village of Ampleforth or Oswaldkirk, and some reports have even stated that Halliwell's father lived at one time just a few streets away from where Claudia went missing. The father and son were close, so whilst Halliwell's father would not have been in the area in 2009, having died in August 1992, Halliwell would have known the area from his time there in the past.

The university lake is stocked with fish, and seasonal fishing is permitted with a licence. We believe that in considering a keen fisherman such as Christopher Halliwell as a suspect, an area of this lake should be searched by the police's underwater team. We also established that Monk Bridge on the River Foss is a two-minute drive to Claudia's address and is about the same distance if you track Claudia's intended pedestrian route. The Foss is a tributary of the River Ouse and draws in visitors due to its passage through the city of York. As well as having an attraction for boaters, The Foss is also popular with anglers; it contains several species of fish including Pike, Dace, Chub, Gudgeon, Perch and Roach.

Witnesses in Claudia's case have also mentioned a man fitting Halliwell's description to the police, as well as vehicles that may be of interest in relation to the ones registered to him. The description of a left-handed smoker, 5ft 8-10in, with slightly receding hair and a skinny build spotted on Claudia's route to work matches Halliwell.

In Karen Edwards' book *A Killers Confession*, she says that she was contacted by a woman in the north of England who told her about a believed sighting of Halliwell in York about two weeks prior to Claudia going missing as her daughter was walking home after her night shift.

This woman described to Karen how, early one morning, her daughter had seen a vehicle parked with its engine off and no lights on, describing it as an old type Rover. When the young woman had passed the car, which was parked near a bus stop, she could see a man inside and the man leant across towards the passenger side and stared at her. She described him as having the most evil stare. His movements in the car frightened her and she hurried off. She thought it very odd that he didn't pick up anyone from the factory and that he was just parked up watching. Once she arrived home, she phoned her mother as the incident had frightened her. She reported the incident to the police when she heard of Claudia Lawrence's disappearance, and they took a statement from her back in 2009.

When Halliwell's face appeared in the local York press following his trial for Becky's murder in 2016, she rang her mum, saying: 'I swear that's him, that's the man in the car that morning near Nestlé, he had the same face the same piercing eyes.'

This witness contacted the police again in December 2016. At the time of this second contact, the witness was told by police that Halliwell wasn't in York at the time she described. It is unclear why they could be certain about this, especially so long after the events took place; they were not aware of Halliwell at the time of Claudia's disappearance and are reluctant to link him to the case, so we wonder how they are in the position to refute any sightings of him?

Whilst researching this book we were contacted by another witness who believes she also saw Halliwell, but was likewise dismissed by the police when she contacted them. She told us she felt like North Yorkshire Police dismissed her sighting as 'insignificant' because Halliwell is behind bars and that she was made to feel as though they didn't want to know. The witness told us that she saw Halliwell on 14 March 2011, and again a few days later on the 16th or 17th of that month. This was just days before Halliwell abducted and murdered Sian O'Callaghan.

Our witness first saw the man she believes was Christopher Halliwell on the 14th at the Kilburn White Horse, which is a hill figure cut into the hillside in the North York Moors National Park, near Kilburn in North Yorkshire. She spoke to him in the car park there, telling us she feels foolish now for opening up to him about an accident she was recovering from and telling him where she worked, but the conversation had just flowed.

A few days later, she was at work in Pickering, a town on the border of the North York Moors National Park, when a taxi pulled across the entrance. She said this was strange, as either side of the doorway was a pallet, so with this silver car parked there no one could get in or out easily. The woman described how the balding, skinny guy she had seen a few days prior at the car park of the White Horse called her over, telling her he was called Christopher but saying 'call me Chris'. She said that he had told her he was an independent minicab driver who was there to tout for taxi business and asked her to put his business card on the staff notice board.

The pair chatted for a while, the taxi driver telling our witness that he was staying with friends for a while with a view to moving north permanently and that he was from Swindon. She told us that a few of the things he said to her were strange, things like 'you have lovely green eyes and a smile that reminds me of my mother' and she described his eyes as 'pale blue ice diamonds' that looked straight through her, continuing to say, 'they are weird, they kind of draw you in'.

When she returned to the office her co-worker ripped up the business card in a fury, saying the man was someone she thought would be a suspect in Claudia's case. She believes that a co-worker had contacted the police but that the garden centre's CCTV only showed her and didn't cover the area with the taxi so they were unable to see the man she was speaking to.

Our witness had attempted to contact the police to discuss whether or not the vehicle she saw the taxi driver called Chris driving was one registered to Halliwell, but had not had any responses.

The witness also told us about a rucksack she knew of that was found on the bank of the River Derwent in Malton. A thirty minute drive from York, Malton is a market town in North Yorkshire. The witness told us about how the bag was found by a man who noticed it whilst some council workers were clearing the banks of the river, and he reported this finding to police because it resembled the description of Claudia's rucksack. Inside were a number of items that pointed to it being her missing bag.

The man who found the bag took it to Pickering police who said they didn't have the facilities to store it so he went to Malton. Whilst the police did look into this, and did take some items as evidence, our witness doesn't know whether there was a follow up to this finding.

Was Halliwell returning to the area on a visit to a deposition site of a previous victim, as he did with Becky? Was he perhaps returning to the site where he had buried Claudia two years prior? The distance between the Kilburn White Horse and York University is thirty-two miles, as is the distance between the White Horse at Uffington, Oxfordshire, and Swindon. There is also the chance he was visiting the deposition site of Donna Keogh (discussed in Chapter Ten 'The River Tees and Yorkshire Murders') who went missing but has not been found. Also discussed in Chapter Ten is the case of Vicky Glass. The distance between Danby, Vicky Glass' deposition site, and the Kilburn White Horse is also thirty-two miles. The Kilburn White Horse is just six miles from Ampleforth and nine miles from Oswaldkirk, towns Halliwell's father is believed to have lived.

The date 19 March, believed to be of significance due to a breakup Halliwell previously had, ties in with this case, as well as with Linda Razzell's case too, discussed in Chapter Six. Sian was abducted and murdered on this date, and in September 2016 an article was published in the Guardian in which Karen Edwards publicly said she believed her daughter's killer could be linked to the disappearance of Claudia Lawrence as she had gone missing exactly two years before he abducted Sian. Karen told the press: 'I believe he has been up and down the country murdering young women. Serial killers are usually triggered by dates. That was the day that Halliwell broke up with one of his partners.'

The police were able to determine that the car discussed on the BBC Crimewatch appeal, the silver Ford Focus hatchback that was seen driving along Claudia's street, had been manufactured between 1998 and 2004. It would be interesting to know whether a silver Ford Focus is one of the vast number of vehicles registered to Halliwell.

Karen Edwards reportedly told Claudia's mother Joan Lawrence that Christopher Halliwell had been seen with Claudia before she disappeared in York in 2009. In a report by *The Mirror Online*, Karen said a witness said he saw Halliwell talking to Claudia through a taxi window, and that apparently, she had asked him if he had change so she could ring her dad from a phone box.

Wiltshire Police did a CCTV trawl in an attempt to refute the allegation that Karen Edwards, and Steve Fulcher had put forward about evidence of a connection with Christopher Halliwell and Claudia Lawrence's disappearance. It was their bid to satisfy Karen that the information she had received, from witnesses who had approached her, stating that they saw someone matching Christopher Halliwell's description in proximity with Claudia Lawrence, was false. Wiltshire Police identified Christopher Halliwell on CCTV at a Swindon petrol station during the evening of 18th March 2009 and showed the CCTV still to Karen Edwards in a session they arranged between Wiltshire Police and North Yorkshire Police. Steve Fulcher confirmed this to us by email, although he was unable to be more specific about the time. Far from disproving the idea that Halliwell was in York the following morning, this actually indicates that Halliwell had the means to abduct Claudia – the drive from Swindon to York would take around four hours, and so refuelling the car in the 'early evening' would mean he had the fuel to make the journey and plenty of time to get to York, ready to intercept Claudia at around 5am on the 19th.

Claudia's disappearance fits Christopher Halliwell's pattern of behaviour, abducting women walking alone either late at night or early in the morning. Claudia, like Becky and Sian, was slim and petite, which fits with Halliwell's victim 'type' and the fact that she has never been found may well be down to Halliwell's skill at disposing a body. As we saw with Becky, Halliwell was able to bury her in a place that meant she was not discovered for eight years, and even then, it was only because he had shown police where she was.

The police have admitted that there are similarities with Claudia's case and the murder of Melanie Hall, as discussed later on in this book in Chapter Five 'The West Country Murders' but have not yet found direct evidence to link them.

We suggest that Claudia knew Halliwell in some way, and that on the morning of her disappearance she left for work as planned but was intercepted by him and the pair were spotted by witnesses at the side of the road talking, and perhaps arguing. Whether it was voluntarily or under duress we cannot say, but we propose that Claudia then left with Halliwell in his vehicle and that, shortly after leaving with him, he murdered her. As previously discussed, in both murders that Halliwell was convicted for, he moved between county boundaries, so there is the chance that Claudia is buried somewhere away from York, out of North Yorkshire Police's area of operation. Another plausible theory is that she was submerged in York University Lake, as with Maria Christina Requena, whose case we will discuss later in Chapter Seven 'The East Lancs Ripper'; she was discovered in Pennington Flash Nature Reserve.

Chapter 5

'The West Country Murders'

As we have mentioned, after leaving school, Christopher Halliwell moved to the West Country and in the 1980s he served his sentence in HMP Dartmoor, and was released in 1987. From this point on he lived at a number of addresses in Swindon. On his release from prison, Halliwell worked as a window cleaner and soon met his future wife, Lisa Byrne, who was, at that point, aged 16, while Halliwell was in his early 20s. The pair later married during 1991. They were together for over a decade and had three children. By his own admission, Halliwell had one-night stands throughout their relationship, being the charming 'ladies' man' he was, and he also admitted that he would pay for sex from local sex workers while they were together. Indeed, Becky Godden-Edwards was one such young woman, as was an unnamed sex worker who provided testimony in court for Halliwell's trial for Becky's murder.

We have looked into a number of cases which appear to have links with various canals and waterways throughout England which Halliwell could have accessed at the time, as well as those which match up with his *modus operandi* in the two murders for which he was convicted and his victim type. This chapter contains cases that centre around the West Country, a loosely defined area of south-western England comprising Wiltshire, Gloucestershire, Cornwall, Devon, Dorset and Somerset.

Eila Karjalainen

Late in August 1983, a Finnish hitchhiker called Eila Karjalainen left London and travelled to the West Country. Eila had arrived in England from Finland on 2 August 1983 and was planning to see as much of the country as she could by hitchhiking her way around during a two week holiday before she returned home to start a course in mental health nursing. The young woman had met a lot of people in London, recording their names and information in her diaries that she carried with her. She was last seen on 7 August 1983 in London, heading west on the A40 to Oxford, and failed to return home to Helsinki as planned on August 14.

It is unclear why she had travelled to Woodstock, Oxfordshire, but there is a theory that she was headed to a Barry Manilow concert that was taking place at Blenheim Palace on the 27th of that month. What happened in those weeks is unknown, and Eila was not seen again. Her body was discovered on 25 November in King's Wood on the Blenheim Estate in Woodstock. She had been strangled and left naked, aside from her socks, in a shallow grave. The area in which she was found is secluded, a woodland filled with copses and lush greenery. This young vibrant woman had come to England for an adventure before beginning her training course and had hitchhiked around, making many friends along the way, whose names and information she recorded in the diaries she carried with her, but tragically met such a brutal end.

Blenheim Palace is a World Heritage Site with over 300 years of history. It is known for being the birthplace of Sir Winston Churchill, and is the home of the Dukes of Marlborough, as well as a popular tourist attraction that draws people in from across the globe. The palace, park, and gardens are open to the public, there are areas on the grounds for fishing, and five miles of public rights of way through the Great Park area of the grounds. The area in which Eila was found is so remote that it meant she went undiscovered for three months. Three weeks after she was found, Eila's rucksack and some belongings, including her passport, were found just five miles away in a layby beside the A40 at Bernard Gate near Oxford. When we follow the direction in which Eila was last seen, heading away from London to her final resting place, and then the dumping place for her rucksack, this route suggests to us that the fleeing offender was heading south west; this direction leads towards Swindon.

The failure to catch Eila's killer was a great frustration for Thames Valley Police, who had very little to go on in the way of clues to what had happened to her but continued to look at similar cases in the hope they could solve her murder.

In 1987 Eila's case was re-opened by Thames Valley detectives in searching for the killer of 17-year-old Rachel Partridge, who was murdered at Shaw's Field Farm, Chinnor Hill. Rachel had also been strangled and had been hitching a lift home from a party, so the cases were similar, and police thought there was the potential that they could have been linked.

When Eila's case was re-opened, Detective Sergeant Henry Wymbs of Thames Valley Police told the *Oxford Mail*:

> Murder is the most serious crime. All the resources are immediately put in - but most are solved quickly. If there are no leads and the enquiries show all the suspects have been eliminated, there's no point keeping people on it for the sake of it. We store all the information on a computer, which can be updated at any time - even in 20 years. If a similar type of crime is committed in another police area, we can liaise with them with a view to tying it up.

In 1989 Rachel's family received some closure and justice when, following a cold case review by the Thames Valley Police Major Crime Review Team, Ronald Cheshire was convicted of Rachel's murder.

However, frustratingly for the team investigating Eila's murder, they were able to determine that Cheshire was not responsible for Eila's murder, leaving her case unsolved.

The police continued to focus attention on Eila's murder and in 2000, new technology became available which gave them the opportunity to take fingerprints from Eila's rucksack, diary and travel documents and compare these with a national database. Police felt that one of the biggest mysteries in the case was that some pages were torn out of Eila's diary, the diary she had written names and information in about the people she had met on holiday. There were all the usual appeals for information, the police reported that they had done all they could to find out what had happened to Eila, but no conclusion was reached. It was deeply frustrating for the team who so badly wanted to solve the case.

A few years later, in 2007, it was reported that Thames Valley Police had created a special squad, the Dedicated Review Team, which was comprised of eight detectives. This squad was created to work on the unsolved murders and rapes that had occurred in the previous twenty-five to thirty years in the county of Oxfordshire. They were hoping advances in forensics and DNA analysis, changes in the law and new leads would finally lead them to catch those who had slipped through the police net during previous investigations. Eila Karjalainen was referenced alongside this report in the media.

Detective Superintendent Barry Halliday said to the *Oxford Mail*:

> Murders and sex offences are the types of crimes that have the most impact and the consequences are severe for all those concerned. The public need to have confidence that when they're told a case is never closed, it actually isn't ever closed. It's important for us to try to get some closure for surviving families and victims. Even if we find we can't progress a case further now, it will be reviewed again in two years' time.

At the time of Eila's discovery, and in 2007 when the Dedicated Review Team was established, the police did not have Halliwell on their radar, so we suggest that he is looked at now by the Dedicated Review Team as a suspect in this case. A lone hitchhiking woman would have been an easy target for him, she wouldn't have needed persuading into the car as she was happy to hitchhike, and her deposition site was one that was so remote she was not found for three months, suggesting a killer who would do his best to hide a body well.

We propose that Halliwell offered the hitchhiking young woman a lift, after spotting Eila by chance, perhaps sexually assaulted her, and, as with Becky Godden-Edwards, strangled her, before hiding her body in a manner that would avoid discovery for a long time and disposing of her belongings along his route back home.

Shelley Morgan

Shelley Morgan was born in 1951 in Iowa, United States, and was creative from an early age; according to her sister, she loved designing and making her own clothes and creating elaborate stuffed dolls and animals. At the age of 17 she was accepted into the American Field Service foreign student exchange program, which gave her the opportunity to spend the summer living with a family in Japan. Shelley continued to embrace this sense of adventure, going to college to get a degree in theatre arts, taking a summer internship in her second year at an opera house in Rome, and the excitement of all this travel confirmed to her that this was what she wanted to do. Fiercely independent, Shelley began looking around for employment in Europe, knowing her dream home would be in England, and soon she was offered a job.

Shelley emigrated to the UK in 1972 to work as a wardrobe manager for the Liverpool Playhouse, turning her love of fashion and design into a career. A while later she met Nigel, who she married, and the pair moved to Nigel's hometown, a small village in South

Wales where they had two children. Enjoying the slower pace of life in the village, the family had a lot of friends in the small community, but when their son was diagnosed with a form of autism, they chose to relocate from South Wales to a new home in Bristol, hoping to find better educational and therapeutic opportunities for him. Whilst they missed their friends, the move was a good one for the family as their son flourished in his new surroundings.

Although she loved her life as a mother, busying herself with her children and their hobbies, Shelley continued to express a desire to return to work as a designer. She planned to finish her arts degree and began participating in art classes at Bristol's Polytechnic Art College, taking advantage of the time her children were in school to do this.

On Monday, 11 June 1984, Nigel was at the family's second home in the Brecon Beacons, approximately two hours away. Shelley was at home, getting the children ready for school. At about 8.30am she walked the pair to their bus stop as usual and dropped them off like any other day. The children recalled their mother telling them she planned to spend her day taking photos and sketching in the Avon Gorge area.

She promised to pick them up from school later and said her goodbyes. Carrying a distinctive multi-coloured carpet bag containing a camera tripod and 35mm Olympus OM20, and wearing unique red-rimmed glasses, the artist waved goodbye to her children, heading towards the picturesque area where the River Avon runs through limestone cliffs. Nearby is the popular tourist attraction of the Clifton Suspension Bridge, featuring several beautiful parks and lots of picturesque natural areas.

When she did not return as planned to collect her children at the end of the school day, the police were called and a search began. It was totally out of character for Shelley to vanish. A friend told the Bristol Post: 'She's a very capable and caring mother, and a cheerful person with no worries. Shelley took the children to school and home again every day She is not the sort of person to go off.' The friend also added that Shelley was unlikely to have gone off with a lover and left the children to fend for themselves.

Avon and Somerset Police began to piece together Shelley's movements and were soon able to confirm that she had caught a local bus from Bedminster's East Street to the bus station early that morning, before most probably boarding the number 359 country service bus to Portishead, twenty minutes away. They wanted to find the driver of a blue van who was seen speaking to Shelley on the day she disappeared at a bus stop near the entrance to Ashton Court, ten minutes from East Street, as well as a woman who may have got on the same bus as Shelley.

Some callers responding to the police appeals reported the sighting of a woman sat inside a yellow lorry, and others spotted a BMW car parked on the Portishead-to-Bristol road, but the leads never amounted to anything and neither did the appeals. By late August, the police were no closer to finding her. They tried a final appeal to attempt to jog someone's memory with a segment on BBC's Crimewatch, and plastered the streets with 200 posters. They even played a recording of a call they had received that September, a call in which an anonymous caller told police that Shelley's body would be found in a 'watery grave' and named a specific location. Their searches had turned up nothing, and detectives were sure it was a hoax, but they wanted to cover all bases. Sadly, none of these leads yielded any clues.

Finally, on Sunday, 14 October 1984, Shelley's family got answers at last, but not the sort they had hoped for. Her naked skeleton was discovered by a boy in a wooded copse off Long Lane in Backwell Hill, near Bristol Airport. If she had arrived at her Portishead destination, as suggested by the bus police thought she had taken, her final resting place was a twenty-five-minute drive away. If she had made it to the Avon Gorge to sketch, this is a fifteen-to-twenty-minute car drive away.

Shelley's remains were found with just a pair of torn and twisted tights around her ankle bones. A pair of sandals was found discarded in brambles nearby. The remains were confirmed as Shelley's by dental records, and a forensic post-mortem examination revealed she had been stabbed in the back fourteen times in a brutal attack described by the police as sexually motivated.

The discovery of Shelley's body prompted a renewed investigation by Avon and Somerset Police and further appeals. But by March 1985, no closer to identifying her murder, the incident room was closed down. The police were not willing to stop searching for answers though, and the case was kept open with a team of six detectives. Police continued to appeal for help, stating their belief that Shelley's killer must have had access to a vehicle and that he may have had links through work or other associations to Bristol.

Shelley's murder remains unsolved, but the crime not forgotten. As recently as 2019, on the thirty-fifth anniversary of the murder, Avon and Somerset Police made a refreshed appeal. As part of this appeal, detectives released images of two postcards which they said may have a significant bearing on their investigation. The tear-off postcards are from a calendar sold by the local Bristol Hospice charity in the 1980s or 1990s. One postcard is of a scene overlooking the River Avon in Bristol, and the other is of St Andrew's Church, from the direction of Backwell Hill. Both locations are significant as they are linked to the areas where Shelley was heading on the day she disappeared and where her body was found five months later. Police were keen to speak to anyone who may have bought this calendar or who kept the tear-off postcards with these specific images, and the appeal did generate a number of calls, but still no resolution.

So why should Halliwell be looked at as a suspect in Shelley's murder? One of Halliwell's itinerant occupations was as a refuse collector and the area where Shelley Morgan's remains were deposited overlooks a landfill site which he would have had knowledge of. He had access to a vehicle and is known to have had links with Bristol as well as a good knowledge of this area. Neither Shelley's camera, her bag, or the clothing she was wearing, including the unusual, red-framed glasses, have ever been found. Shelley's camera may have been of value to a thief like Halliwell as an item he could very well sell on, and her clothing may have been taken as a trophy. Once again, we think that it is shocking that the police have still not made their findings from the Ramsbury area public; perhaps one or more of these items would be found within the sixty recovered from Hilldrop Lane.

The deposition site at Backwell Hill is situated just over four miles and a ten-minute drive from the very popular fishing site of Barrow Gurney Reservoir.

Not only does Shelley's murder fit with Halliwell's *modus operandi*, but Halliwell also had an interest in sketching. When he was arrested for Sian's murder, a number of Halliwell's sketches were taken by the police, but the content of these has not been disclosed. Halliwell was also known to be charming and a persuasive conversationalist. Knowing the River Avon and the Kennett and Avon Canal system well from his social activities as a freshwater fisherman and narrowboat enthusiast, he would easily have been able to strike up a conversation with Shelley about a number of topics, if the conversation hadn't flowed from their shared interest in sketching.

We would suggest that not only should the stash of clothing items from the Hilldrop Lane pond be checked for Shelley's missing items, but that Wiltshire Police should reveal to the public the sketches made by Halliwell in their possession in another public appeal; after all this could be a potential lead in helping to solving this case and bring closure for Shelley's family. Perhaps he sketched the area where Shelley had been abducted, or the area in Backwell where she was later found. After all these years with no resolution, what has Wiltshire Police got to lose?

Linda Guest (also known as Jackie Waines)

On Sunday, 22 April 1985 a young couple were taking a shortcut along a bridlepath. The shortcut, near Frampton Cotterell, a village in South Gloucestershire, is known locally as Lovers Lane. It was 12.30am when they came across a shocking scene of a woman lying on the ground in a gateway to a field. The pair rushed to the nearby Perrinpit Farm, and awoke the homeowner saying that they thought there had been a rape. The homeowner went with them to the scene, but sadly the woman they had stumbled across in the dark was not alive after all.

The woman they had found was Linda Guest, sometimes known as Jackie Waines. The 35-year-old mother-of-three was a sex worker who worked from the St Paul's area of Bristol. Subsequent investigations showed that Linda had been sexually assaulted and stabbed to death with her blue and white striped mini dress left in disarray. One of her shoes was missing and she had been left lying in the gateway in a pool of her own blood. The shoe was never found. The place where Linda was found was close to the M4 motorway to Swindon and was around eight miles from where she lived in Hepburn Road, Bristol.

The last sighting of Linda was at 11.10pm on Saturday 21 April 1985 in Ashley Road, 1 hour and 20 minutes before her body was found. This was a regular spot for Linda when working the streets and was close to where Linda lived in Hepburn Close and where she usually took her clients. The last time she was seen alive, she was walking down the road in the direction of her home.

Neighbours said Linda was a quiet woman, sometimes described as a loner, who kept to herself. Indeed, she had only one real friend, a woman who she shared a house with. Linda had lived at a home in Bevin Court for around seven years, and had shared the home with her family, a husband and three daughters. But after her husband left her and the girls were taken into care, Linda had moved in with this friend. She had kept hold of the maisonette, still collecting her post from there in the morning, but it was separate to her new life and new choice of employment.

Avon and Somerset Police detectives were eager to work out whether Linda had been picked up in a car or had an appointment with a man the evening she disappeared and appealed for witnesses. Naturally, given this was the city's kerb-crawling hotspot, people were not eager to come forward, but the police continued to appeal for any information. Detective Sergeant Malcolm Hughes, who led the investigation, said: 'I would like to emphasise that we are not looking to prosecute anyone for prostitution. Our priority is to catch a brutal murderer.' Police focused their search on the possibility that Linda was picked up by a client and released pictures of the only clues they had to Linda's final movements. These photos showed a shoe Linda had been wearing that night, and a white van. The other shoe from the pair Linda had been wearing was missing and was never found.

In July 1985, a re-enactment was shown on BBC's Crimewatch. The re-enactment took the viewer through Linda's last known movements the night she was killed, showing Linda getting into a red Cortina car with a man with blond curly hair and later talking to the driver of an Escort-type van. It also showed that at roughly 12:10am, four young men were parked in a vehicle at the so-called Lover's Lane, listening to music and blocking the entrance when they saw a white van pull up and the driver leave a large white bundle on the floor, something they assumed was an act of fly tipping. Around 120 phone calls came in as a result of the show but led nowhere.

The white van is of key importance in this case. A couple in a car had seen a white van parked on the corner backed into the lane with a young, slim man standing by it with his back to the road, wearing a checked lumber jacket. By 12:15am both the van and the man in the jacket had gone. Other witnesses described a white two- to three-ton van, with plain sides, no windows and some damaged paintwork on its offside. This was a similar description to the one seen in the lane, and this van was said to have been spotted around Frampton Cotterell at about 12.10am. A similar vehicle was seen at a nearby junction at around 1.40am. Witnesses said that the driver was a slim man, aged between 20 and 40, with short, dark hair, which fits the description of Halliwell at this time.

Linda's case had the benefit of being investigated in one of the very first 'computerised' investigation rooms. This meant that use of the then brand-new HOLMES system, a computer system providing total compatibility and consistency between all the Police forces of the UK. HOLMES, the Home Office Large Major Enquiry System, was introduced in 1985 and enabled law enforcement agencies to improve effectiveness and productivity by processing the mass of information it was provided with. Avoiding human error, using this system ensured that no vital clues were overlooked. But by early autumn, officers had followed up 3,400 lines of inquiry and taken 1,850 statements from the public in relation to Linda's murder yet, despite the sophisticated technology available to them, the police were still no closer to catching her killer.

Flowing through the village of Frampton Cotterell is the River Frome. During the relevant seasons you can catch salmon, sea trout, brown trout and grayling on the twenty-mile-long river, making the numerous fishing spots along the way popular for anglers. Linking the village to Bristol, it may have been a river Halliwell knew well. The large white bundle that the man with the van was spotted placing on the ground was more than likely Linda's body, as this is where she was found shortly afterwards. There is a pond at the end of Perrinpit Lane and we believe it was the intention of Linda's killer to drive in and leave her there in the water, but that he was disturbed and was forced to flee instead. A deposition site such as this, with the body submerged in water, would help to disguise a number of forensic clues. As the information relating to the disposed of items at Hilldrop Lane is not public knowledge, we have no way of knowing whether Linda's shoe is amongst the sixty or so items that were recovered. There is also no way of accessing the information relating to the vehicles registered to Christopher Halliwell, in particular white vans, but we feel that it is an area of the investigation that warrants further review. We appeal to Wiltshire Police to be transparent with the information they have, as this could help to finally solve this crime.

Carol Clark

It was a pretty standard Friday night on 26 March 1993 when Carol Clark changed into her working clothes; a blue denim mini skirt, short cowboy boots and a baseball hat set at a jaunty angle. She headed out to the red light district of St Paul's in Bristol, just around the corner from her home. Her hair was styled in her trademark style, a long plait. Carol had thought it would be a busy night for her as a sex worker, but actually the night was quieter than she hoped, so Carol headed home. Her partner, Brian, had gone out clubbing with his friends, but rang home as the pair had planned at 12.30am. During the call, Carol said she was hungry and asked him to bring her a kebab when he came home. Brian agreed and assumed she would be there on his return, but shortly after Carol decided to try for one last shot at making some money. At 1.30am on Saturday, 27 March, she headed back out into the night.

Arriving home at 2.20am to find the flat lights on, Brian found a note written by Carol before she left at 1.30am, explaining her hopes of finding a last client that evening. She said in the note that if she was successful, she would be back at 2.30am, but if not, she'd return at 2.10am. When she still hadn't come home by 4am, Brian reported her missing to the police.

Carol Heather Clark was born on 27 August 1960 in Kingswood, Bristol, and had grown up in Yate, Gloucestershire, the youngest child of parents Peter and Phyllis Clark. She dreamed of modelling and travelling and at the age of 17, she left home to work in a Bristol hotel. Sadly, Carol turned to heroin and crack in her early twenties and soon began working on the streets to pay for her addiction. In January 1993, Carol moved in with electrician Brian in his basement flat. Brian knew what Carol did for a living and supported her, although he wasn't totally on board with it. Charging £20-£30 for a 'quickie', Carol went by the names Kate or Charlotte and tended to go with her clients to their cars; she never took her work home.

Detectives learned that Carol needed her methadone on time, or she could pass out and stay unconscious for hours. As a result, when she did wake, she would become angry and violent. She also suffered from epileptic fits, occasionally falling into a deep trance without warning. She would tell Brian where she was, as she did that fateful night in her note, and if she didn't return on time, he would go out and look for her. Whilst her boyfriend wasn't completely happy with her choice of work, he did his best to protect her and support the woman he described as 'independent', the woman he loved who wanted to keep control over a part of her life.

Two days after she disappeared, Carol's partially clothed body was found thirty miles away in a remote area of Sharpness Docks in Gloucestershire. Her body was found in an area known locally as the Swan's Nest, a wasteland that was, although an isolated part of the docks, plainly visible from any passing boat. Carol's killer had carried her from the road over ten yards of rough grass and thrown her down the four foot canal bank. A large scale police investigation was launched by Gloucestershire Police.

The post-mortem revealed Carol's neck had been compressed by a forceful blow; there were no other marks on her body and the attack appeared to have been so sudden, and that she had not tried to defend herself. She was found wearing her bra and pants, although both were in disarray, and still with her boots on her feet. The brown leather jacket, her polo neck sweater, denim mini-skirt and the baseball cap she wore that night have still not been found.

Following appeals to witnesses, a picture of Carol's last hours was built up by the police. The driver of a broken-down car saw Carol talking to a man in a white Peugeot at around 12.15am on Saturday. The coroner looked at what Carol's last meal had been, eaten approximately two hours before her death. The meal had contained diced potatoes, meat and peas, and they surmised that it had been some form of pasty. But the hours between the last definite sighting of her on the streets of Bristol and the time her body was discovered at 4pm on Sunday,

28 March confused the police. Carol hadn't planned to stay out all night because she hadn't taken her methadone with her, and without her fix, she would have known she would be ill with withdrawal symptoms. She had also never previously stayed overnight with a client, so a decision like this would have been totally out of character.

Carol's murder was highlighted on a BBC Crimewatch reconstruction later that summer, her desperate family pleaded for help to find her killer, but there was still no breakthrough for the police and her bereaved family, as hoped. The reconstruction, as well as describing Carol's final moments, discussed how she would usually plait her long blond hair to leave a braid down her back, a braid threaded through her baseball cap. The reconstruction also showed a couple who had been spotted on the Saturday morning in a car in a lay-by close to where Carol was discovered the following day. The woman was described as having blonde hair in a plait and wearing a baseball cap. The witness said she was getting out of the passenger seat of a battleship grey Volvo in Sharpness Docks looking like she had just woken up. This was described by police as a potential last sighting of Carol. They said that perhaps she had fallen into a deep sleep due to her epilepsy and was confused on waking up.

Detective Chief Inspector Wayne Murdock of Gloucestershire Police, who later described the investigation as the most challenging murder investigation in his career, said at the time it was a mystery as to why Carol's body had been taken to Sharpness. But he still held out hope, adding: 'Even now there may be people who can help us. They may have harboured suspicions about someone or a close friend or relative may have confided in them.'

Five years after her murder, and at an apparent dead end, Gloucestershire Police made another public appeal for any information. At that time her father, Peter, said: 'It's not very nice to know that whoever did it is still out there, but the police have not given up hope. The fact that nobody has been caught leaves a chapter unfinished.'

Years later, following the release of ITV drama *A Confession,* which detailed the investigation into Christopher Halliwell and the discovery of Sian and Becky, Carol's brother-in-law was quoted in the papers as saying the family had noticed similarities between the way Carol had been killed and the way Halliwell killed his victims. He said:

> We have never had any answers so if there are similarities between the way Halliwell carried out his killings and the death of Carol, we would urge the police to look into them. We have not heard anything from the police for years so perhaps there could even be a forensic breakthrough they could use now, such as his DNA? It is hard not knowing what happened to a loved one so anything that can be done to find answers would be welcomed by our family.

Investigators believed although she disappeared that night, Carol was not murdered until either late on the Saturday night or in the early hours of the Sunday morning. She was definitely alive late Saturday evening, meaning she had to have stayed or been kept somewhere. Could that have been on board a boat and is that where she had her last meal? That weekend was a busy one, as it was the celebrations of the Bristol and Avonmouth waterways, an event that may well have attracted Halliwell.

Without her methadone, Carol would have been irritable and violent on waking up, and perhaps this was the reason she was killed, perhaps she had made a scene or become aggressive.

As well as being a sex worker, Carol's slim build fits Halliwell's victim type, and the missing items of her clothing have never been found. It would be interesting to know whether her cap, jacket, skirt or jumper are part of the sixty items found in the pond at Ramsbury. Carol kept a journal naming some of her clients, and whilst the police tracked down some of the men named, they were unable to find many others. Would it be possible for the police now to check this to see whether Halliwell's name was in this diary? He would not have been a person of interest at the time of Carol's murder.

Sally Ann John

In a similar manner to the way Halliwell was described as being 'obsessed' with Becky Godden-Edwards, he has also been reported by some witnesses as behaving in the same way towards a young woman called Sally Ann John. Sally was born and brought up in Swindon, had a happy childhood, and like most other young girls she spent time outside riding her bike and enjoying family picnics and trips to the park. She was said to be especially close to her mother. As her teenage years progressed, she became rebellious, and by the time of her disappearance, she was working as a sex worker in Swindon town centre. But Sally maintained a good relationship with her family, especially her mum, and she had a group of friends in the town.

On the night of 8 September 1995, Sally Ann had planned to work until midnight. She was seen in the red light district speaking to police officers that night, although the content of the conversation is unknown. She also spent time catching up with friends, talking to them for a while. She was last seen at 10.50pm, but nobody knows what happened after that. Her disappearance was initially treated as a missing person inquiry as there was nothing to suggest anything more sinister had happened to the 23-year-old. Although the original missing person investigation concluded in 1995, Sally remained a missing person on the Wiltshire Police database.

When detectives revisited Sally Ann's case as part of a review in 2013, they could find no evidence to suggest that she was still alive. There had been no bank account activity in Sally Ann's name and she had not had any contact with the police since going missing. She had not been in touch with any of her friends and family, and so a murder investigation was launched. Sally Ann's mother, Lesley John, told BBC Crimewatch: 'It is a horrible feeling that your daughter has been murdered, I just want her found. I want whoever did this to be held to account for it.' The police searched her last-known address in Swindon, and in September 2015 two men from Swindon, aged 50 and 52, and a 52-year-old man from Chippenham were arrested on suspicion of kidnap and murder. However, all three were later released, and nothing further has developed in her case. The police have not released any information to the public about how these men were initially linked to Sally Ann, or anything further about the charges brought against them. Sally Ann John's body has never been found.

A postcard was received by a male friend of Sally Ann's three weeks after she went missing, which appeared to have been sent by Sally Ann herself, from London. In the post card it claimed she was safe and well, living in London. It read:

> Dear Clive,
> Thought I would write as I've heard you've been missing me, and you were rather worried that something had happened to me. As you can see, I am in London now. But no one compares to you big boy,
>
> Love Sally xxxxxx

For a long time this was an assurance that Sally Ann had chosen to head to London.

However, in 2017 the postcard was analysed, and it was determined not to have been written by Sally Ann, mainly due to the way the letter 'e' had been written. Wiltshire Police announced that the note was therefore not the reassurance it should have been. The police stated they believed that whoever wrote the postcard was perhaps misled into doing so, coerced against their will, or that it may have been written by her killer. Our belief is that this was sent by someone who, whilst well meaning, in fact halted what could have been a more thorough investigation by allowing the police and Sally Ann's loved ones to believe she was safe.

In February 2017, it was reported that the police were searching in gardens and garages at two properties in Broad Street, at a home where Halliwell had once lived. This is just a three-minute walk from Aylesbury Street where Sally Ann was last seen, and we know Halliwell had lived in a number of other properties in Swindon. People who knew Sally Ann have said that Halliwell, at one point, lived in a flat in Aylesbury Street where she was working when she went missing.

Speaking to *The Mirror* in 2017, Sally Ann's former housemate Sally-Anne described an interaction she had with Halliwell prior to leaving Swindon and her life as a sex worker. Sally-Anne said she had been picked up by Halliwell for sex in his car, but when he put his hands around her neck she fled. She told the paper: 'I can't put my finger on it, but there was something about him I didn't like. He put his hand round my neck in a way that creeped me out and made me scared. I told him I wasn't doing business with him and got out the car. He drove off and I walked all the way back into Swindon. That was the only time I remember seeing him.' She later realised it was Halliwell when she saw the photos of him in the press. Sally-Anne moved to London, leaving her life as a sex worker behind, five months before Sally Ann vanished, and she had tried to get her friend to join her, but Sally Ann didn't want to leave, and the friends never saw one another again. Sally-Anne had no idea Sally Ann was missing until police investigating the disappearance arrived at her workplace asking whether Sally Ann had joined her in London. She has said that she has reported suspicions about Halliwell to the police.

Sadly, as her body has never been recovered, we fear Sally Ann encountered the same fate as Halliwell's other victims. As Halliwell knew the red light district of Swindon well, was known to use the services of sex workers, to drive them around in his capacity as a taxi driver and was believed to have lived in the same street as Sally Ann at one point, there is a lot to suggest he knew her, at least by sight if not better – perhaps they had a relationship similar to the one he had with Becky, where Halliwell felt he had some sort of right to her and wanted to keep her for himself. Naturally, he wouldn't have been on the police's radar as a suspect in 1995, and they didn't open the investigation up to murder until a lot later, but it would be revealing to know for sure if Halliwell did in fact live at an address in Aylesbury Street at a similar time to Sally Ann. Even without this information, it is telling that Halliwell lived just five minutes away and was known to use the services of sex workers in the area.

Melanie Hall

On Saturday, 8 June 1996, Melanie Hall headed out with her boyfriend and friends for a night in Bath. The last time she was seen alive was at 1.10am, sitting on a stool at the edge of the dance floor at Cadillacs nightclub.

After thirteen years of anguish for her family, Melanie's remains were discovered by a workman in October 2009, in woodland near Thornbury, a market town in South Gloucestershire, about twelve miles north of Bristol and around a forty-five minute drive from the centre of Bath.

Melanie Hall was aged 25 at the time of her murder and was a clerical worker at the Royal United Hospital in Bath. Described by her parents as a 'young, vibrant daughter', she had graduated from the University of Bath the previous year, something she had worked hard towards and had dreamed of doing; her mum said graduation had been a 'cherished' dream of Melanie's for four years. She had arranged to stay at her boyfriend Dr Philip Kurlbaum's house on the night of her disappearance, and her mother had dropped her off earlier that day. The pair hadn't been together very long, only a few weeks, and had met whilst both working at the same hospital. They had headed out into town with another couple and went to Cadillacs nightclub, described as the 'place to be'. But the night took a turn for the worse when an argument ensued between the couple after Philip thought Melanie was dancing with another man. He left the nightclub upset, although he hadn't told anyone, so when Melanie's friends decided to leave to head home, they believed they were leaving the pair together.

What happened in the hours that followed is not known, despite numerous appeals and witness statements. Melanie was reported missing to the police by her parents after she failed to turn up for work on the Monday morning. Avon and Somerset Police launched several searches of the River Avon after her disappearance, made appeals, interviewed thousands of clubbers and taxi drivers, and worked tirelessly to try and find Melanie, but she appeared to have vanished into thin air. A reward of £10,000 was offered for information, and appeals were made on BBCs Crimewatch and Crimestoppers.

Two families who lived very close to Cadillacs nightclub came forward to say that they had heard what appeared to be a screaming woman. They had apparently heard the words 'Leave me alone, let me go' on the evening that Melanie disappeared, but this lead didn't amount to anything.

In the BBC Crimewatch reconstruction from November 1996, there were reports of Melanie being in the company of a young man inside the club and later when leaving at around 2am. Two witnesses came forward to say that a young woman matching Melanie's description was seen arguing with a man outside the Church Hall, and there was also a sighting of a woman of her description in the company of man trying to steer her into the Paragon Car Park which is adjacent to the River Avon Canal.

We believe that this sighting in the car park is significant, along with other information received regarding a narrowboat moored in Bradford-upon-Avon on 16 June 1996, where a couple were overheard discussing someone called Melanie. Both are pointers towards Christopher Halliwell who was unknown to police forces at that time.

The man was described as in his late twenties (Halliwell would have been aged 32) with an approximate height of 5'10', a medium build and very suntanned, and this description fits Christopher Halliwell from that time.

Six months after Melanie had disappeared, her boyfriend, Dr Philip Kurlbaum, was arrested. Whilst he was being questioned, police carried out forensic searches of his car, but ultimately, they found nothing that could link him with his girlfriend's disappearance. Over the years, eleven people were arrested but no one charged. There was a campaign launched by the police in 2006 to find a sporty white hatchback Volkswagen Golf. Sadly, this lead appears to have been a dead end for police.

Although she had officially been declared dead five years earlier in 2004, hope remained in Melanie's family that, by some miraculous chance, she might turn up alive one day. That painful desire was wiped out on 5 October 2009 when a worker clearing a vegetation patch on a slip road at Junction 14 of the M5 Motorway made a gruesome discovery. They had found a plastic bin bag containing what they suspected were human bones. The bones in the bag were confirmed to include a skull, pelvis and thigh bone and when the police searched the surrounding area, further remains were subsequently found buried and spread around the field by the side of the motorway.

Avon and Somerset Police confirmed officially that the remains were human, and they showed a piece of jewellery found at the site to Melanie's parents, who told detectives that it had belonged to their daughter. A post-mortem had been carried out, and the remains were officially identified as Melanie's through dental records on 7 October 2009. She had incurred severe blunt trauma to her head resulting in a fractured skull, cheekbone and jaw and had been tied up with a blue rope. This blue rope is particularly significant as it was similar to mooring rope for tying up narrowboats, something that would have been easily accessible to him if he was the man spotted with the narrowboat moored nearby.

Melanie's parents launched a fresh appeal on 8 October 2009 for anyone with information to come forward, and Avon and Somerset CID Detective Seargent Mike Britton even stated that he was staying on after his retirement, wanting to solve the crime having spent thirteen years on the case. At the end of October 2009, the police announced that three keys to a Ford vehicle, possibly a Transit, Fiesta or Escort had been found near the body. There was a fresh appeal on BBC Crimewatch, and the reward for information leading to arrest was increased to £20,000.

The police reiterated that Melanie's clothing and accessories were missing; namely her pale blue silk dress with a round neck, black suede mule shoes with straps across the front and an open toe, a cream single-breasted, long-sleeved jacket and a black satchel-type handbag. The handbag had contained cosmetics and a Midland Bank cheque book and bank card, as well as items of jewellery, including a Next watch with expanding bracelet and silver drop earrings.

None of the items have been found, again perhaps some or all of these items are included in the large selection found in the pond and surrounding areas at Hilldrop near Ramsbury.

It is our opinion that Melanie was abducted after leaving Cadillacs Nightclub, as we know that a woman of her description was seen arguing with a man outside the Church Hall, and a woman of her description was also seen in the company of man trying to steer her into the Paragon Car Park. As this is adjacent to the River Avon Canal, we believe it is reasonable to suggest Halliwell may have had his narrowboat moored there, and that the boat may have been the abduction site and crime scene where her body was cut up.

On the evening of Sunday 16 June, a couple walking down the towpath of the Kennet and Avon Canal at Bradford-upon-Avon, Melanie Hall's home village, walked past a dark blue coloured narrowboat with a beige interior and they overheard a couple in their late twenties/early thirties discussing someone called 'Melanie'. The man was stripped to the waist. It would be beneficial to know more about what boats Halliwell had available to him at this point in 1995.

The Kennet and Avon Canal is a waterway in southern England with an overall length of eighty-seven miles, made up of two lengths of river that are linked by a canal. After the opening of the Great Western Railway it was mainly unused and fell into disrepair in the late 19th and early 20th centuries. Later in the 20th century it was restored, mainly by volunteers and was fully reopened in 1990. It has been developed as a popular tourist destination for boating, canoeing, fishing, walking and cycling, and is also important for wildlife conservation. As we have previously said, Christopher Halliwell was both a narrowboat and fishing enthusiast; the Kennet and Avon canal was his local.

In addition, close to where Melanie's remains were left is Heneage Court, a Grade II courthouse within private parkland that includes paddocks, pastureland, woodland and, most importantly, a fishing lake.

Heneage Court is situated on the edge of the village of Falfield in the centre of the Berkeley Vale. The popular market towns of Thornbury (five miles away) and Wotton under Edge (six miles away) provide for everyday requirements and are all located between the River Severn and the Cotswold Hills Area of Outstanding Natural Beauty, providing a variety of stunning landscapes in a relatively small area. The property is located close to Junction 14 of the M5 which is about four miles from the Almondsbury interchange, providing excellent links to the West Country, South Wales and London via the M4 corridor.

Avon and Somerset Police believe it is likely that the person who dumped Melanie's remains knew the area well and could have turned off at the next junction for Dursley or at Michaelwood Services on the M5 before using a slip road behind the services to head back in a southerly direction, which would lead them to the M4 motorway and Bristol.

In his book *Catching A Serial Killer*, Steve Fulcher states:

> Whilst in prison on remand Christopher Halliwell's telephone calls were monitored and in one, he said, "The police want to interview me for eight murders".

His search history exposed an interest in murder, violent sex and rape, and he had a particular predilection for bondage, internet searches on how to tie knots. That snagged my attention: there was an unsolved murder in Bath where the victim Melanie Hall had been tied with a blue rope and I wondered if Halliwell could be a potential suspect in her case. Was Melanie Hall one of the six? [Taking out Becky and Sian from the eight].

Avon and Somerset Police have said Halliwell is not to blame for Melanie Hall's murder, but they have not elaborated on why they are convinced by this, and the accusation has never been put to Halliwell. In the words of Fulcher: 'How can you be happy it's not him? You're supposed to keep an open mind.' In an interview with the *Sunday Express*, Steve Fulcher stated he believed Melanie Hall's murder had similarities to those of Becky and Sian, saying: 'The circumstances match his modus operandi in abducting a girl, late at night, from a nightclub. Evidence of her being tied up with rope is consistent with Halliwell's interests.'

On 4 October 2019 in an article by *Bath Echo*, Senior Investigating Officer Detective Chief Inspector James Riccio, of the Major Crime Investigation Team, said:

As part of a nationwide appeal issued on the 20th anniversary of her disappearance, we confirmed we had recovered DNA on an item found at the site where Melanie's body was found. Today, we're confirming the DNA traces were found on a length of blue polypropylene rope which was wrapped around thin black bin liners which had contained her body.

We recovered a 13-metre length of 4mm rope from the scene, made up from four separate lengths knotted together. In addition to the three knots joining the ropes, there were four other knots on the rope – a total of seven knots.

It's commercially manufactured rope and commonly used on building sites and for drawing electrical cable through trunking. Do you know someone who was in possession of blue polypropylene rope which went missing in the summer of 1996? It's possible their behaviour or demeanour may have changed since this date. Did you have this type of rope which inexplicably went missing in the summer of 1996?

Detective Chief Inspector James Riccio continued:

We believe the choice of deposition site is key. Whoever left Melanie's body in the undergrowth off the northbound slip road of junction 14 of the M5 would have done so in haste. It would have happened on the morning of 9th June 1996, or within a few days of this date. It's likely this person would have then driven onto the northbound M5 and either onto the next junction, or they may have turned off at the Michaelwood Services, where they could have used the local road network, including a slip road behind the services, to head back in a southerly direction. We believe it's highly likely the person who left Melanie's body at this location was familiar with this area.

From the BBC Crimewatch reconstruction and the witness statements, and knowing what we do about Halliwell's motives, methods and history, it is credible that he could be responsible for her abduction and murder. She was walking alone, late at night, after leaving a nightclub in an area Halliwell knew well. Melanie fits Halliwell's victim 'type' and he would have had the means to transport her, whether by narrowboat or by motor vehicle. Not only this, but he would have had access to narrowboat rope and be knowledgeable in knots. Melanie's remains were not found for thirteen years, showing her killer had hidden her in a skilled manner in a deposition site well chosen, and items of her clothing have never been recovered. These thoughts have been passed on to the joint Avon & Somerset / Gloucestershire / Wiltshire murder investigation team, with a suggestion again that the clothing and items found at the pond at Hilldrop Lane in Ramsbury be checked, but we have frustratingly received no response.

Earlier on the day that Melanie went missing, events occurred which may have been a catalyst for Melanie's abduction and murder. These will be discussed in Chapter Twelve, 'The Bath Rapist'.

Three missing women: Sandra Brewin, Tina Pryer, Thi Hai Nguyen

As well as Swindon resident Sally Ann John, there have been other women who have seemingly vanished without a trace in Halliwell's local area of Wiltshire, but sadly with these three cases there is very little to go on with investigating their disappearances. Due to the lack of information, we are unable to do much more than speculate, but with so little to go on we feel the potential link to a convicted murderer from the area should be explored further. It is important that they are remembered and discussed.

In 1994, Sandra Brewin went missing from the home she shared with her parents in Peatmoor, a popular area of Swindon a fifteen minute drive west of the main town centre. The 21-year-old had become penfriends with a man who was in prison in Oxfordshire, her parents believed, but it isn't known who this was.

Tina Pryer was 39 years old and working as a cleaner for University of Bath when she vanished on 15 April 2001. She was last seen getting into a taxi near her hometown of Trowbridge, Wiltshire. Was this taxi Halliwell's? He may well have picked up this job, as Swindon and Trowbridge are only thirty miles apart, or perhaps he was her regular driver if she often took taxis.

Thi Hai Nguyen went missing from her home in Marlborough, Wiltshire, on Friday, 14 October 2005. The 20-year-old Vietnamese woman had only been in the town for a matter of weeks. At the time it was thought that she had simply moved on to another city or perhaps had even travelled back home, so her disappearance was not widely publicised or appealed.

The bodies of these three women have not been found.

As mentioned, there is very little that has been reported on with these three women and, as far as we can tell, there have been no updates or renewed appeals over the years. Steve Fulcher has also been vocal in the media, stating that he believes that Christopher Halliwell murdered Sandra Brewin. We believe the disappearances of these three women should be looked at in much more detail by Wiltshire Police in relation to Halliwell as, whilst he was not a suspect at the time they went missing, this convicted murderer lived in the area at the time the women vanished.

We suggest that the police forces should be looking into the items of clothing that were found at the pond at Hilldrop, Ramsbury, to see if anything matches the missing items of clothing mentioned here in this chapter. We would also suggest the vast number of vehicles registered to Halliwell are checked for the makes and models noted by witnesses in these cases.

The women in this chapter who went missing from the West Country could have been killed by Christopher Halliwell and then buried somewhere remote and unknown, remaining undiscovered, as in the case of Becky Godden-Edwards before Halliwell led police to her body.

Had it not been for Steve Fulcher getting Halliwell to take him to Becky's remains, and the police's efforts to identify her, Karen Edwards would still be driving around Swindon at night hoping to find her daughter, wrapping up birthday and Christmas presents with the hope she would return. How many other families could Halliwell bring closure to if he admitted to these potential murders too?

75

Chapter 6

Linda Razzell

Linda Razzell, a 41-year-old teaching assistant, went missing in 2002. She lived in Highworth, a market town and civil parish in Wiltshire, about six miles from Swindon town centre. Her husband Glyn is currently serving a sentence for her murder, although he continues to protest his innocence and her body has never been found.

Linda and Glyn had first met on a train in 1979. Linda was from Llanybydder in Carmarthenshire, Wales. She was studying French and Italian at Reading University and he was starting out in a career in insurance. They were soon married, eventually having four children, and the family lived in Highworth, just outside Swindon. Their marital difficulties began when Linda had an affair with a builder who was working on an extension to their home. When Glyn found out about the affair in 2000, he left and soon started up a new relationship but the couple's four children stayed with their mum. Linda also found a new partner, Greg Worrall, and eventually the Razzells decided it was best to divorce.

Sadly, friends of both have commented on how bitter and protracted the relationship had become between the two. The divorce proceedings were fraught with arguments; Linda made two allegations that Glyn had physically assaulted her. Both times Glyn was acquitted in court.

Linda and Glyn's divorce was due to complete in July 2002. Glyn was set to take a significant financial hit with the separation as his was the higher paying job and Linda earned a lot less than him. When he was made redundant, Glyn stopped paying Linda maintenance money. Four days before Linda disappeared, she was granted a court order which froze all of Glyn's personal bank accounts, due to this non-payment of maintenance. The day before Linda went missing, Glyn's solicitor advised him to attempt to get this decision overturned in the courts.

On Tuesday, 19 March 2002, Linda Razzell left her home in Highworth at around 8.40am and drove the seven-mile journey to Swindon for her job at Swindon College. After dropping her boyfriend at work and children at school, she parked her car on Alvescot Road in a residential area and began heading to work on foot, as she did every morning, but this morning she was running late. Usually Linda parked her car for work at about 8.45am, before walking to the college. The walk would usually have taken Linda about twelve minutes to complete, and on the morning in question Linda was spotted at just after 9:00am, entering an alleyway on her usual route. She didn't make it to the college and has not been seen since. The alarm was raised when she failed to pick up her two youngest children from an after-school club, and an investigation was started.

In the weeks that followed, Wiltshire Police appealed for information, released CCTV images and took statements from witnesses. There was also an emotional witness appeal made by Linda's estranged husband, Glyn, and her current boyfriend, Greg, with both men pleading for information. Greg said later in the press that they had planned to marry as soon as Linda had divorced Glyn, and that she was wearing his engagement ring when she disappeared.

Greg, who worked at Honda, had begun to worry after Linda failed to return any of his calls; he had sent a series of texts and even phoned Swindon College where Linda worked, but had failed to get through on each occasion. Linda had dropped Greg off as normal that day, albeit a little late, and he had gone to watch Linda's youngest son in a school assembly later on, but he hadn't heard from her through the day, assuming she had left her phone in the car. He then began to worry that something much more serious had happened when he got the call to say Linda had failed to pick up her children their after-school club, so he left work early. The co-owner of the after-school club was quoted as saying, 'Linda was always on time to collect them, I never knew her to be late'. Greg phoned the police later that day. At around 10pm Greg went out to look for Linda. He found her car, still parked in Alvescot Road, but no sign of her mobile phone or Linda herself.

It was a shock to the public when the police charged Linda's estranged husband with his wife's murder on 17 May 2002. The arrest came after police became increasingly suspicious of Glyn who gave incorrect information about what he was wearing on the day Linda went missing and gave 'contradictory statements' about his whereabouts.

On the Monday before the morning in question, Glyn had made plans to join friends on a trip to France. The group were due to leave on the Tuesday morning, however, due to the divorce proceedings, his solicitor had advised him that he may be required in court relating to the freezing of his bank accounts, and so he pulled out of the day trip. Glyn, who owned a Ford Galaxy, had agreed to exchange cars with his friend's Renault Laguna, just for twenty-four hours, to allow his vehicle to be the one used for the trip, even though he couldn't go. He spent the following day, the day Linda went missing, staying close to home, going for a walk some time during the morning.

As police began their initial searches, they located Linda's mobile phone in the same alleyway she was last spotted walking towards. Just after 1am, Wiltshire Police arrived to speak to Glyn and, as well as asking him questions, they also searched his car, which had just been returned to him. Glyn told the officers that he'd been using a different car, his friend's Renault Laguna, during the day. The next afternoon, the police searched the Laguna. They didn't find anything suspicious on the first search and so they kept it for four days while they carried out a second, more thorough, examination. Again, there was no evidence whatsoever to connect that car with Linda's disappearance.

As time went by, police began to get more suspicious of Glyn's actions after they realised that he had provided incorrect information about what he was wearing on the day of Linda's disappearance. They had returned the Laguna to its owners but decided to run a third search of the car due to their mounting suspicions about Glyn and his story. On this third search the police found spots of blood that DNA testing subsequently showed to be Linda's.

Let's look at the timeline of these three searches. The car was first forensically tested for blood on 20 March, using intensive light treatment. The Scenes of Crime Officers (SOCO) took forty minutes on the Laguna, using four different techniques, and found no sign of blood or recent cleaning. On 21 March, the car was taken away to the police garage where two officers spent five hours working on the car and a full scene of crime forensic examination was done. Tapings and swabs were taken but all results were negative. No hair, skin or blood was found. The car was given back to the owner and, at this point, the owner of the Laguna chose to get the car thoroughly cleaned as the police had returned it to them in a filthy condition with fingerprint powder everywhere. He said he cleaned the boot but did not notice any marks. On 28 March, the car was inspected by the police for the third time and it was at this point that blood was detected using a chemical test called Luminol. Blood was found in the boot and there was a small mark on the passenger's footwell mat.

Forensic scientists said, at the time, that there were heavy blood stains, visible to the naked eye. No one has ever been able to explain how those original two police searches of the car could have missed these very obvious bloodspots. Glyn's defence claimed that the blood was planted. No blood was found elsewhere in the car; there was no blood on the driving controls, the door handle or on the lip of the boot. There were no hairs, skin, clothing fibres or fingerprints matching to Linda in the car.

No blood or any other forensic evidence relating to Linda was found at Glyn's house or on anything else seized from Glyn.

Even the waste traps were taken from the bath, sinks and washing machine. Waste traps are used to provide a water seal to the drains or atmosphere, for all water using appliances and fittings within a house. They provide a water seal, preventing smells, bacteria and insects entering the property, but would also keep miniscule evidence traces for the police to investigate; all the waste traps taken from the home came up negative.

There is a lot of doubt about whether Glyn Razzell is responsible for Linda's murder after all, and he continues to maintain his innocence whilst in prison. We, of course, do not know the truth, however there are a lot of parts to Linda's case that ring alarm bells and seem to point to Christopher Halliwell as a genuine suspect, which raises concerns about whether Glyn Razzell's conviction is safe.

As is often the case, there were a lot of local rumours about what had happened to Linda. Some people speculated that she had chosen to leave of her own accord, whilst others wondered if she had chosen to fake her death to frame Glyn. But the key rumour was that Linda knew, and was potentially in some sort of relationship with, Christopher Halliwell. As well as both being from the same locality, Linda went missing on 19 March, which is a date we know is of significance for Halliwell as the date he had a major breakup in the past.

Incredibly, two witnesses have reported to Karen Edwards, Becky's mum, that the pair were having an affair. These witnesses have also stated that Halliwell acted obsessively about Linda, going as far as to sit in his car opposite the alleyway through which Linda would walk to work, the alleyway where her phone was found following her disappearance. Wiltshire Police have commented on how there may be possible links to Halliwell, and they state that these links continue to be investigated, however, it seems that to this day that the two witnesses who spoke to Karen Edwards have not had their statements taken by the police.

On the kitchen calendar at Linda's home, there was a question-mark against the 19th, the day on which she disappeared. There were a few things that were strange about Linda's behaviour that day; she had to wear a college identity badge to work but had left it at home, and she also had a second mobile phone purely for contact with her children, but this was also left at home and there has been no reason given for why this was.

Glyn took a quick two-minute telephone call at home at 8.24am from his girlfriend, who had just arrived at work. Of course, this call would have been on a landline phone, not a mobile, so it ties him to the property at such a key time. Where Glyn lived was about fifteen minutes from where Linda went missing, and even though Linda was running late on the morning of the 19th, Glyn would not have known this. She would usually have needed to park her car for work at about 8.45am, so surely if Glyn had been planning to intercept his wife, he wouldn't have taken that phone call at home.

Wiltshire Police examined traffic cameras at twenty-five sites to find evidence of Glyn's potential drive across town, but the car Glyn was using that day wasn't spotted on any of them. He told the police that he had an alibi for his walk that morning, as he had actually passed a police station. He told them: 'Look, on my walk I went past Westlea police station. There are CCTV cameras outside, so you will be able to verify what I am saying.' Frustratingly, the CCTV cameras outside the station were not working that morning and therefore could neither support nor refute Glyn's claims. There were three cameras covering Glyn's route; two of these, including the one at the police station, were not recording, and the third was not seized promptly and, consequently, the tape was reused and the evidence lost.

In September 2002, Glyn appeared at Bristol Crown Court and pleaded not guilty to his wife's murder. He was bailed and the judge adjourned the case until the following summer. The main motive given for Glyn's guilt was money; he would have profited from his wife's death. The Crown claimed that Glyn stood to benefit from a substantial amount of money if Linda died. However, there is evidence to prove that Glyn knew Linda's will had been changed to leave all of her assets and money to the children, and that he was aware that Linda's life insurance pay-outs would also go to the children. In addition to this, Linda had taken steps to change the ownership of their house so that her share would not go to him in the event of her death, something it was rumoured that Glyn knew.

At the trial, the prosecuting barrister put it to Glyn, 'I suggest you killed your wife for the two oldest reasons there are – money and a younger woman who you were in love with. That's right isn't it?' but Glyn simply replied, 'No, that is not right' and continued to protest his innocence.

After a month-long trial, Glyn was found guilty of murder at Bristol Crown Court on 15 November 2003 and was sentenced to life imprisonment. This remains only one in a handful of UK cases where a murder conviction has been granted despite the body of the victim never being found.

Glyn Razzell's parole hearing was set for the summer of 2021, after being delayed during the pandemic. In October 2021 the Parole Board refused his release on the grounds of the Prisoners (Disclosure of Information About Victims) Act 2020, known as Helen's Law. This states that those who are convicted of murder should not be considered for release if they do not reveal the location of their victim's remains. At the time of this book going to print, Glyn remains in prison.

The police have said that there may be possible links between Halliwell and Linda's disappearance and that they will continue to investigate these links. They have also been quoted as saying that none of those clothes found in the Ramsbury pond had been linked to Linda.

But, as Steve Fulcher says in his book *Catching a Serial Killer*, 'The point is, there are witnesses who have come forward to say a convicted killer and a missing woman were in a relationship, and nobody in the police force have taken their statements. They have therefore de facto suppressed something that might undermine the safety of a conviction of a person serving a life sentence.'

Circumstantial evidence certainly seems to suggest that Halliwell could be responsible for Linda's disappearance and that it is not unreasonable for this to be investigated further. This is a missing woman whose remains have never been found, who went missing from the town where a man who would later be revealed to be a murderer lived. The claims by witnesses who have said they would see Halliwell waiting in his car 'obsessively' for Linda at the alleyway through which she would walk to work, the alleyway where her phone was found following her disappearance, plus the claims made by people who state the pair were in a relationship need to be investigated fully.

Chapter 7

'The East Lancs Ripper'

Within this chapter we will be discussing six cases from the area known as the 'Liverpool / Rainsford / Leigh / Manchester Quadrilateral'; these are cases including murders and a missing person's investigation. Halliwell had lived in the Liverpool area, so would have known it well and his hobbies centring around fishing and narrowboats may have led him to the Leeds and Liverpool Canal for leisure and recreation.

The Leeds and Liverpool Canal goes from Liverpool, passes close to Rainford, then to Wigan and on to the Pennington Wharf Marina at Leigh, where it becomes the Bridgwater Canal. The Bridgwater Canal then joins the Rochdale and Ashton canals which are in the city centre of Manchester. This canal network contains abduction points, disappearance points and deposition sites from the cases discussed in this chapter. The crime scenes concerned are clustered around four points on this canal system that it is likely Christopher Halliwell knew well.

The chapter title 'The East Lancs Ripper' refers to a cluster of murders suspected to be the work of a serial killer dubbed as such in the press. The phrase 'East Lancs' refers to East Lancashire, an area in North West England, which includes Manchester and Liverpool. The cases grouped together in the media are those that concern Linda Donaldson, Maria Christina Requena, Julie Finlay and Vera Anderson. However, we do not personally feel that Vera Anderson's murder is linked to the others. We will discuss her murder towards the end of the chapter to explain why. Officially, Greater Manchester Police and Merseyside Police have never formally linked any of these cases.

The Angel of the Meadows

The first woman in this cluster of cases is a still-unknown woman who has been nicknamed the 'Angel of the Meadows'. Estimated to have died in the 1980s, but not discovered until 2010, this unidentified woman was found in Manchester city centre.

On 25 January 2010, at a site in Miller Street, workmen helping construct the Co-operative Group's new £100m headquarters discovered a human skull. They contacted the police, who attended the site and a skeleton was unearthed.

The remains had been wrapped in carpet, and police stated that at first the discovery was not classed as suspicious, however, as the post-mortem results came in, the police investigating soon realised this wasn't an old skeleton, but rather a much more recent murder victim. The post-mortem showed that the woman had suffered a fractured neck, collarbone and jaw. Further examination showed that she had been sexually assaulted and stripped prior to her death.

As we saw with Becky, when the Angel of the Meadows was found there was a lot of discussion in the media about her potential identity. There was speculation as to whether this was the body of Helen Sage, a missing woman we will be discussing later on in this chapter, but this was disproved when the victim's dentistry did not match Helen's dental records.

The land where the skeleton was found is a redevelopment site located between Angel Street, Dantzic Street and Miller Street. The area is known as Angel Meadow, and it used to be a notorious Manchester slum in the mid-19th century. It was famously described by Friedrich Engels as 'hell upon earth', and it was sadly the final resting place for this woman who had met such a savage end.

Greater Manchester Police were able to establish from a specialist who carried out Carbon-14 testing on her teeth and bones that the woman had been born sometime between 1950 and 1954 and was aged between 18 and 30 when she was murdered. The woman had been between 5ft 1in and 5ft 8in tall and was a UK clothing size 12. They determined that she was probably European but could have come from the Middle East or Indian sub-continent.

Alongside the skeleton, police found a bra, tights, a pinafore dress and jumper. It is believed the clothing belonged to the woman, but she was stripped before her body was dumped. There was one black high-heeled shoe alongside the remains, but the missing shoe was never recovered. Was this taken as a trophy by her killer? There was also a handbag but this was empty.

Three different colours of carpet were found at the scene – orange, blue and dark blue. The blue carpet appeared to have been cut to fit a Ford Cortina, with holes for a gear-stick. Some of the carpet was burned, meaning there may have been a fire at the site, and that perhaps the killer had tried to remove forensic evidence. This is indicative of Christopher Halliwell and the forensic awareness he showed and actions he took when he killed Sian O'Callaghan.

Greater Manchester Police investigated possible killers known to have operated in the area, and considered two convicted murderers and one serial rapist as suspects, but none of them have been charged.

Ronald Castree was one such suspected killer; the convicted murderer had fatally stabbed 11-year-old Lesley Molseed in Rochdale, Manchester in 1975, although he wasn't caught until thirty-one years later. A local man named Stefan Kiszko had been wrongly charged with Lesley's murder, and in what has been described by one British MP as 'the worst miscarriage of justice of all time'. He was found guilty and went on to serve sixteen years in prison for this crime he did not commit. Castree was finally convicted of the murder in 2006.

The second man Greater Manchester Police looked into was Peter Tobin. The Scottish serial killer and sex offender is currently serving a whole life order for three murders committed between 1991 and 2006, and prior to this he served ten years for a double rape committed in 1993.

The final man was known prior to his arrest as the Rotherham Shoe Rapist in the media. James Lloyd was arrested in 2006 and pleaded guilty to four rapes and two attempted rapes, and was sentenced to fifteen years in prison. His *modus operandi* included stealing the footwear and jewellery from his victims to keep as trophies. Lloyd was known to be active during the 1980s.

The police were unable to find links or evidence to prove any of these men were the murderer of the Angel of the Meadows.

Greater Manchester Police worked tirelessly to try to identify the woman, asking the public for their help, and featuring the case on an episode of BBC's Crimewatch on 24 May 2011. This feature also included a facial reconstruction that scientists had created of the woman, and this was published in the papers across the country. Using DNA, they checked missing person reports and at one point had managed to narrow down their searches to twenty-two possible women.

One witness believes he may have met with the woman later known as the Angel of the Meadows, having spent time talking to a woman he felt was scared by something or someone, when they met in a bar in the early 1970s. When Alec Whittle saw the news articles, he recognised the pinafore dress that had been found as one he had seen then, and was convinced that the woman he spoke to that night, who he remembers being 'afraid', is the same woman whose body was recovered at Angel Meadow. He contacted police in 2010. Police say they fully investigated the information Alec put forward at the time. Aside from this, over the years, sadly, no one has ever come forward with definitive information about who the woman was.

Five years after being discovered, in March 2015, the Angel of the Meadows was laid to rest in an unmarked grave in Southern Cemetery, Manchester. She received a funeral paid for by the state and there was a quiet service that was attended by two of the Greater Manchester Police detectives working her case.

In 2017, the head of Greater Manchester Police's cold case review unit, Martin Bottomley, said they would 'never give up hope' and he told the BBC: 'She deserves a proper burial, which she's now had, and she also deserves justice. There will be a family member out there somewhere who knows who she is and who can unlock that key and identify her and perhaps that will lead to the murderer. We are determined to get a just outcome for the victim, and for any family member out there, and we will never give up hope.'

In 2021 a gravestone was made for the Angel of the Meadows and flowers were laid at her grave in her memory.

The main similarity with the case of the Angel of the Meadows and Christopher Halliwell's actions following his abduction and murder of Sian is that Halliwell had taken the time to burn the seat covers and mats from his car; the carpet used to transport the Angel had been destroyed also. The deposition site at Angel Meadows is just over half a mile from the Rochdale Canal, which connects the Leeds and Liverpool Canal via the Bridgwater Canal, and the site is also half a mile from the River Irwell, two well-known fishing spots popular for a keen angler. Whilst only circumstantial evidence is available to us in this and indeed many other cases, and the cases remain officially unsolved, the above suggests that Christopher Halliwell is a viable suspect as the murderer of the Angel of the Meadows and his movements at this time should be investigated.

Linda Donaldson

There were two confirmed sightings of Linda Suzanne Donaldson before she was murdered. The first was at roughly 11pm on Monday, 17 October 1988 by a Merseyside Police vice squad officer who knew many of the women working in Liverpool's then red light district. The second was at around 1am on the morning of Tuesday, 18 October by a sex worker. Linda was also a sex worker; she lived a transient lifestyle and was sharing a flat with friends in Canning Street at the time of her death. It is not known for sure what Linda did between the two sightings of her on her final night on earth. She was found dead the following day, brutally murdered, with her killer barely trying to hide her body.

Linda Donaldson had been born in Liverpool on 22 January 1957. Linda's mother Elaine was young, aged only 15 when she had her daughter, and she had some problems of her own, so she asked her mother to look after the baby and gave Linda her maiden name. Linda's father was reportedly from another country and never knew his daughter. Linda's grandmother Emma brought her up and, by all accounts, her childhood was a good one. She did not know who her mother really was for a long time and it was believed that at the time of her death they were not in contact. When Linda left school, she decided to study hairdressing. At the age of 18 she got married, but the relationship, which was childless, didn't last and the couple separated.

Sadly, for Linda, the break-up affected her badly. She fell in with a rough crowd and, along with her boyfriend, she turned to drugs, soon becoming dependant on these and shortly afterwards she turned to sex work to feed her addiction to heroin. The pair lived in a commune in Holland for a while before returning to Liverpool, but sadly this relationship didn't last either and in 1984 they split up. After the split Linda was able to stay with different friends on their couches for a time before moving into her flat in Canning Street. She had pets that she and her flatmate had rescued as strays and has been described as loveable.

Linda was no stranger to the police having been in court for charges relating to personal possession of drugs and prostitution, but people who knew her have said that she was not a nasty, violent, or mean person. The local sex workers liked her and described her as caring and one of the men who had paid her for sex said that she was a friendly woman with a great personality.

On the night that she was last spotted, Linda was working close to her home on Canning Street. Canning Street, three miles from the Liverpool end of the Leeds to Liverpool Canal, is close to Albert Dock. There is a stark contrast between the darkness of the red light district of the city and the glamour of Liverpool's historic waterfront filled with museums, restaurants and culture, but the Liverpool of 1988 was very different to the Liverpool it is today; now a bustling cosmopolitan city, it was at this time a city fraught with union disputes, unemployment and recession.

Linda was wearing her usual characteristic style of black clothing; a black jacket, black skirt and black ankle boots, plus a studded belt and gold earrings that have been described as distinctive. None of these items, or her white address book have ever been found. She had left her flat at around 11.30pm and was spotted by a local policeman sometime between then and midnight. There was also the report that another sex worker had spotted her at about 1am, but after this point there were no more sightings of Linda. When she failed to return home the following day her flatmate reported her missing to the police.

Linda's body was found some twenty miles away in Winwick Lane in Lowton, a village in Greater Manchester. It was at noon the next day on Tuesday, 18 October that an elderly couple were travelling along the remote stretch of road and pulled over for the man to relieve himself in the bushes. He was shocked to discover that in a gully close to the field side of the hedge lay the mutilated body of a woman. Whilst the location where Linda's body was found is isolated, the road leads north to the East Lancashire Road and south to a junction of the M6.

The post-mortem examination would later conclude that she had died from multiple stab wounds. The pathologist determined that Linda was dead before a lot of the injuries had been inflicted, including trying to sever her head from her body and the mutilation of her breasts. Linda had died from two stab wounds in the back but there were eight others in her body, all inflicted after death.

Linda's elderly grandmother who had raised her had the awful task of identifying the body; Emma was able to confirm that this was the body of Linda Donaldson by a scar on her earlobe. Linda's body had been washed down before being dumped, seemingly in an attempt to remove forensic evidence by her killer.

As we know Christopher Halliwell is incredibly forensically aware, having been caught cleaning and burning items in an attempt to remove any trace of himself from Sian's murder. Linda's killer attempted to remove forensic evidence with water. This crime also follows Halliwell's pattern of abducting female victims from one police force area and dumping them in another. Similarly, in the case of Becky Godden-Edwards, her skull and arms were missing when the remains were excavated by police and it appeared the same had been attempted on Linda.

Speaking at the time of the murder, Greater Manchester Police Detective Chief Superintendent Ken Clarke said: 'We are looking for a maniac - a sadistic killer who could strike again. The type of man who could do this to another human being defies description. The mutilation was probably done in a bid to conceal identity.'

The police were aware that although she often had regular clients, Linda was not averse to picking up strangers either and so their assumption was that she may have got into the car of a kerb crawler. It was of course also possible that she got into the car of a familiar client. The police were sure that she had been driven away and killed at another location by whoever had taken her.

The police investigated the scene at the field. Tyre tracks could be seen coming off the road and up to a wooden gate near the scene, where they continued on to the gully before looping back round to exit again onto the road. The driver of the car would have had to get out of the car to open the gate and they would also have had to close it again behind them, but frustratingly none of the tyre tracks could help narrow down the search for the mystery vehicle, and there were no clues as to where the car headed after leaving the field and re-joining the road.

From the very beginning it was going to be a difficult inquiry for the police. The body had been dumped after the murder and so the police did not know where the murder scene was, there was also no murder weapon and no obvious motive for Linda's murder. There had been no sightings of Linda in the hours since she was last seen in Canning Street and the discovery of her body.

Witnesses came forward to say that a maroon-coloured Ford Granada Mark Two was seen parked at the entrance to a field close to where Linda was found. This car was seen at 5.45am some six hours before the body was discovered, and it was spotted at the same place an hour later, but this car was not traced. The European Ford Granada is a large executive car manufactured by Ford Europe from 1972 until 1994. The square and straight-lined Granada Mark II was released in August 1977 and was produced until early 1985, which narrows down the number of this type of car on the roads at this time. It would be interesting to know whether such a car features on Christopher Halliwell's long list of registered vehicles.

The police began house to house inquiries and interviewed everyone known to have associated with Linda. Of course, there may well have been witnesses they were unable to contact, but the police reported that they felt they were lucky that they did not come across any difficulties in getting the sex workers and/or the men who had used the women to talk to them. Whilst this is a nice thought, we feel this shows naivety on the police's part; how would they have known definitively who they needed to speak to and who refused to come forward.

In a kind gesture, one of Linda's clients later anonymously offered a £1,000 reward to catch her killer, but sadly no viable suspects were forthcoming.

A week to the day after Linda was found, police set up roadblocks to interview people who might have been in the area on the morning of Linda's death, but again this was to no avail. The murder was featured on BBC Crimewatch in December 1988, and this episode featured interviews with local sex workers and even a man who had paid Linda for sex on a regular basis who said that although he was initially a client of Linda's, he really did care for her and missed her. The programme also described how at around 11.30pm the night Linda had disappeared, another sex worker had turned down a client because he had made her feel uneasy. The man was unfamiliar to this woman and he was carrying a bag that made a metallic clanging noise that made her nervous, and he asked if she knew of anywhere 'dark' they could go. This woman said she had seen Linda later that night at around 1.00am and had wished her a good night before heading home. She said her last sighting of Linda was her walking towards a dark car in the alleyway, but it's unknown as to whether she thought this was the same car she had seen earlier that had made her feel uneasy. This woman was able to create for the police a photo fit of the worrying stranger, but sadly the trail went cold.

The BBC Crimewatch feature triggered sixty phone calls, but frustratingly to the police there was no breakthrough. Linda's case was highlighted in a number of newspaper articles but, again, despite all the media attention, there were no further leads. Locals worried that her death would not be the only one at the hands of such a killer; many women feared going out at night, and a sense of unease gripped the sex workers of the Liverpool red light district.

Maria Christina Requena

Unfortunately the police and indeed the press and public, who had been worried that the killer might strike again, were proven right when, just over two years later, the dismembered body of 26-year-old Maria Christina Requena was found in five bin bags. Two youngsters fishing on the shores of Pennington Flash Nature Reserve, off Slag Lane, made the gruesome discovery on 6 January 1991. Like Linda, she had suffered a sustained stabbing attack and her head had been removed from her body. The post-mortem examination showed that

Maria's body had been cut up with power tools and placed in five bin bags, before these had been thrown into the lake.

Maria, like Linda, had been a sex worker. She was from Manchester and had also suffered with drug addiction issues. The place where her body was found is within a third of a mile from Leigh Marina, part of the Leeds and Liverpool Canal, and close to the Leigh Waste & Recycling Centre on Slag Lane. She was discovered just three miles from where Linda had been found and the police soon believed the crimes had been linked; not only because the women had been found so close to each other but also because of the way in which they were killed. The women worked in red light districts at either end of the East Lancashire Road, and they were both dumped roughly halfway along the dual carriageway in rural backwaters. Both had been subjected to stabbing attacks; the killer had attempted to decapitate Linda and had cut up Maria, and in both cases water was used, presumably to ensure removal of forensic clues.

Maria was born on 12 June 1964 in the Kensington district of London. She originally worked the Paddington red light district but not much else is known about her short and tragic life. She is buried in the Manchester Southern Cemetery, at grave number FF 699.

In a strange twist of fate, both Linda Donaldson and Maria Christina Requena had appeared on a television show in 1987. They had featured on an episode of Kilroy which discussed prostitution and the issues faced by sex workers. They both opened up about the struggles faced by sex workers who felt they had no other options left to them, often due to their addictions, and on the documentary, Linda described how she wouldn't dream of picking up a man if there were children around, showing her caring and compassionate side.

Julie Finley

On Sunday, 6 August 1994 at around lunch time, a cyclist happened across a horrific scene in a carrot field off the Rainford bypass.

Stopping the bike, they looked closer, and saw in front of them the lifeless and naked body of Julie Finley. The field is just off the St Helens-bound carriageway of the Rainford bypass, just five miles from the Sankey St Helens Canal, and is a thirty-five-minute drive from Liverpool city centre. It was well known as a popular place for fly tipping. Julie had been strangled, there was no sign of her clothing and, according to the police, it was clear that her body had been dumped in the field rather than being killed at the scene.

Julie was the second eldest of five children born to parents Pat and Albie, and a few days prior to her death she had celebrated her 23rd birthday. Julie was believed to be a drug addict who mixed with sex workers and so it is a possibility that Julie had also turned to sex work herself, although this has never been confirmed. The police were unsure where she was living before her death, as she was not living at home with her parents and family. The last confirmed sighting of Julie was sometime between 10.30pm and 11pm on the night of the 5th, near the Royal Liverpool Hospital, once again close to the Leeds-Liverpool Canal. She was seen by some railings talking to a white man, of average build, aged in his twenties or thirties. She had been wearing a white t-shirt at this point.

A core team of fifteen detectives worked on the murder investigation, questioning over forty men who came up as persons of interest to them in the first six months on the case. The police appealed to the public about a white Transit van which was seen by a passer-by near to the entrance of the carrot field where Julie was found. A witness came forward who said he saw someone matching Julie's description arguing with a man at about 12.30am on Saturday the 6th outside the Wheatsheaf Public House. This is just fifty yards from where Julie's body was found the following day. According to the witness, an unknown man was attempting to force this young woman matching Julie's description into a white Transit van.

A woman calling herself Tina had called the police shortly after Julie's murder, telling officers that on the night of her murder, Julie had told Tina of her intention to meet a taxi driver from Prescot. She said that she and Julie had been friends and 'Tina' promised to call the officers back. Sadly, this woman did not leave contact information and, despite pleas from the police, Tina failed to contact the police again.

About ten months after Julie's murder, the police were contacted by a man who said he had picked up a hitchhiker who, on passing the spot where Julie had been found, had become incredibly nervous. The man said that when he asked the hitchhiker about his agitation, the hitchhiker explained that at the time of the murder he had had stopped in a lay-by near to the field because his motorbike had broken down. The hitchhiker continued that he had seen a white van, from which he could hear bangs and screams coming. He went to the rear doors and opened them, finding a young naked woman who said to him 'help me, help me, for God's sake help me' but he said that a man then came over and told him that the woman was his girlfriend and told him to mind his own business and to get away, which the hitchhiker said he did. The police said that as the story had included information that only they knew about, information they had chosen not to reveal to the public or the media, they thought that the account was true, however the hitchhiker himself had never contacted the police directly. It would appear that this hitchhiker was the last person to see Julie Finley alive and he had seen her murderer, however he never came forward to give an official statement.

As far back as September 2014, we tried to persuade both Merseyside, the lead force and Avon & Somerset, the intelligence unit looking at Halliwell's offending, to consider Julie's case as one of Halliwell's. The investigation by GMP hadn't led to any charges, and we would suggest the reason for this is that these women were killed by Christopher Halliwell, a man who was not yet on their radar for investigations. It took a further five years for an article in the *Daily Mirror* and Julie's mother to force Merseyside Police to reinvestigate Julie's murder with Halliwell as a strong suspect. The article described the murders of Linda Donaldson, Maria Christina Requena and Julie

Finley, and added in new information from a witness. This witness said Halliwell was staying in nearby Aughton at the time of Julie's disappearance, where he worked as a window fitter from Monday to Friday, before returning to his hometown of Swindon. The witness also stated that Halliwell drove a white van similar to the one spotted, and that the taxi driver lived just four miles from the field where Julie Finley's naked body was dumped.

The information from 'Tina' about a man known as a taxi driver is significant as, at one time, according to Steve Fulcher, the man who arrested him in 2011 for the original double murder, Christopher Halliwell had lived in the Liverpool area and often his occupation was ground work or taxi driver as he migrated around the country. Not only is this occupation fitting, but all of these abductions and depositions had taken place close to the canal network which is indicative of Halliwell's social life. Whilst the description of the man by some railings talking to Julie is vague, it does match Halliwell from this time; a white male of an average build and the right sort of age range, being as Halliwell would have been in his twenties at this time.

Then, in November 2020, Merseyside Police began a major search in woodland close to Aughton and Julie Finley's deposition site, although Merseyside Police remained tight-lipped about the nature of the painstaking search, with forensic investigators and police officers appearing to dig in a large area of woodland. The area they were searching is close to the roadside on a popular route for drivers heading to the Rainford bypass. The wood is just 4 miles from Aughton Park, Ormskirk, where we now know Christopher Halliwell lived in 1994, but there have been no updates from the police about the outcome of this search.

Helen Sage

In August 1997, Helen Sage went missing, leaving behind her 6-month-old daughter. She has been described as a devoted mother, someone who would not choose to leave her child. Helen was a sex worker in Manchester's City Centre and was last seen in the red light district on Minshull Street.This is the very same area where our previous victim, Julie Jones ,was believed to have worked.

She was, at one time, suspected of being the Angel Meadow murder victim but she was eliminated through dental records. Greater Manchester Police have also not formally linked her disappearance with Julie Jones, although they have recognised that the cases are similar. Helen is still classified as missing.

Greater Manchester Police's Cold Case Unit have stated that due to there not being any physical evidence of her death, Helen's disappearance will not be treated as murder. However:

- There was no known reason for Helen to choose to leave.
- No trace of Helen has ever been found in the years since she went missing (The National Crime Agency has confirmed there is no proof of life).
- Despite being a sex worker at the time of her disappearance, and having no other means of making money, Helen has not once come to the attention of the police since she went missing.
- She left behind her 6-month-old daughter and has not contacted her family.

We are shocked that the police did not investigate Helen's disappearance as a potential murder. Although her body was not found at the time, and there was no physical evidence of her coming to harm, the fact that she left behind a young daughter to whom she was reportedly devoted suggests to us that it is incredibly unlikely that Helen would have chosen to run away..

Greater Manchester police have said of the decision not to open a murder enquiry:

At the time of Helen's disappearance a number of hypotheses were explored to establish what happened to her. As with cases of this nature, this is normal procedure to make sure that every outcome is considered to try and find that person. Helen's disappearance is not currently being treated as murder as there has never been any physical evidence to suggest she was killed. Of course, if any new information came to light, we would review this.

One of the main risks of street sex work is the fact that the women frequently get into the cars of their prospective clients, people who they often don't know. It is very possible that Helen got into the car of her killer, expecting him to pay her for sex, but was instead killed, and this would mean that there was no crime committed in the city centre for the police to find evidence of. It is then also difficult to establish where the crime actually took place, especially as Christopher Halliwell's *modus operandi* is to drive his victim to a remote area.

Not having a body does not mean that a disappearance may not be treated as a murder. Throughout this book we have presented cases that are similar in nature to Helen's; Sally Ann John disappeared on 8 September 1995, but Wiltshire Police reclassified her disappearance as a murder in 2013. The North Yorkshire Police also did this in the Claudia Lawrence enquiry, but there was no physical evidence of a crime taking place in either case. Linda Razzell's husband is serving a life sentence for her murder despite no body being found because the Crown ruled that she would not have abandoned her children and therefore she must have been abducted and murdered and, in fact, this was one of the key factors used to convince the jury of this, even though there was no body.. Following this ruling, surely the same conclusion could be reached in Helen's case. Becky Godden-Edwards' murder was not solved for eight years, and the similarities are quite striking between her case and that of Helen Sage. The absence of a body or any physical evidence should not be used as the sole elimination criteria to automatically prevent the re-classification of Helen Sage's disappearance as murder.

Julie Jones

Some four years after the murder of Julie Finley, a woman called Julie Jones was reported missing by her housemate on 27 June 1998 when she didn't return to her home in Ancoats, in the northern part of Manchester city centre. Julie was a sex worker, and it is believed that she had been working on the night she disappeared. Her usual place of work was around Whalley Range and the area around Minshull Street in Manchester city centre. At the time of her disappearance, Julie was 32 years old, and had two sons.

Growing up in Abergele, Wales, Julie was a popular, academic girl who had a Catholic upbringing and regularly attended Sunday school. She enjoyed netball, singing and dancing, and wanted to work in hairdressing when she was older. When her parents split, she moved to Bury in the North West of England with her mother, continued to flourish, and her life was described as happy. Sadly, at around the age of 28, Julie fell in with a rough crowd, she moved to Manchester city centre and began to take drugs. Julie then turned to sex work to pay for her addictions. Throughout everything, her sons were very important to her so, whilst she used to move around a lot, she ensured her boys were well looked after by taking them to stay with her mother, their grandmother. She would then make sure she made the time to return to see them and spend time with them as often as she could. Julie's sons were 13 years old and 17 months old at the time of her disappearance and at this point they were staying with Julie's mother. Her mother has since said of Julie that 'her boys were always number one'.

Six days after Julie was reported missing, on 13 July 1988, a woman was walking her dog when she discovered, wrapped in carpet, Julie's naked and lifeless body. She had been hidden under bushes outside Old Smithfield Market, which used to be a fish market. The area in which she was found was close to the town centre and to her home. She had sustained severe injuries consistent with being brutally attacked; her injuries have been described as horrific and have been compared to being hit by car or falling from a great height. Julie's clothes and jewellery were never recovered.

Greater Manchester Police investigated and came to the conclusion that Julie had been killed and kept elsewhere before her body was wrapped in carpet and dumped. The police did arrest a few people over the years, but no one has ever been charged with Julie's murder and her case remains unsolved. One person who was arrested without charge for Julie's murder was subsequently convicted of a different crime on a rape charge.

The locality of where Julie was abducted from is significant to us, as it links to Halliwell's interests once again. Minshull Street Bridge straddles the Rochdale Canal in Northern England, between Manchester and Sowerby Bridge, and is part of the connected system of canals of Great Britain. Its name refers to the town of Rochdale through which it passes. The Rochdale is a broad canal because its locks are wide enough to allow vessels of a width of fourteen feet. For boaters, this canal is a peaceful place to escape the crowds, the towpath is a nice easy walking route through the Pennines, taking you into the heart of the hills. The Undercroft – the part of Rochdale Canal which runs underground from Dale Street to Minshull Street – has long been a venue for sex workers picking up clients as well as cruising and dogging. Holidaymakers on canal boats have often complained of seeing people engaged in sex acts as they sail past, and some have said that this is an area that, whilst close to the city centre, is one tourists should approach with caution.

The similarities to these cases and those confirmed to be the work of Christopher Halliwell are striking. Halliwell revealed he had buried Becky Godden-Edwards' body, minus her head and arms, in a field, and we know that there were attempts made to remove Linda Donaldson's head from her torso. Linda and Julie's items of clothing and jewellery were never found, and neither was one of the Angel of the Meadows' shoes; could these personal items be in the collection discovered in the pond in Ramsbury, Wiltshire, where items belonging to Sian and Becky were found?

With Maria's murder, the method her killer used of disposing of her body parts in bin bags is similar to the 1996 case of Melanie Hall, as discussed in Chapter Five of this book, 'The West Country Murders'.

Serial killers prefer to operate in areas that they are familiar with so they know their way around. Halliwell had lived in the Liverpool area and we know that he enjoyed narrowboating and fishing, so it makes sense that he may have spent time on the Leeds and Liverpool Canal, which is just three miles from the abduction points of Linda Donaldson and Julie Finley. Halliwell may also have stayed with his father in the Huddersfield and York areas, giving him a good knowledge of many northern cities and the areas around them.

All three sites where the women had been dumped were in rural areas, which is consistent with Halliwell and the other cases we believe can be linked to him. The site where Julie Finley's body was found is 10.6 miles from the Leeds and Liverpool Canal at Waddicar, 11.7 miles from the Leeds and Liverpool Canal at Wigan and 13 miles from Liverpool City Centre. Alongside this it is probable that Halliwell knew Manchester too. He may have holidayed on the Rochester Canal, which would take him into Manchester City Centre close to the abduction point for Maria Christina Requena and the deposition site of the Angel of the Meadows.

Halliwell worked in dozens of jobs that we know of; he worked as a taxi driver and bin man as well as a labourer and groundworker at different times. Prescot is 6.5 miles from the site where Julie was found, and Tina had said Julie told her she was going to meet a taxi driver from Prescot. This taxi driver from Prescot may have been a regular client of Julie Finley if she was indeed a sex worker. Halliwell was a regular client of Becky Godden-Edwards before he murdered her. All three victims fitted Halliwell's victim preferences, and all were enticed into a car or vehicle. Pennington Flash, where Maria Christina Requena's body was found, is about a mile from the Leigh Waste & Recycling Centre on Slag Lane. Linda Donaldson's body was found about two miles away from it. The Angel of the Meadows fits the general profile and age range for Halliwell's known victims, and there is no way of knowing, until she is identified, whether she had also been a sex worker.

The descriptions of the unsettling stranger that approached the sex worker who knew Linda, and the man Julie was witnessed talking to, are also similar to Halliwell. Firstly, 'A white man, late 20s', and secondly, 'A white man of average height and build, aged in his 20s to 30s.' Christopher Halliwell was aged 30 in 1994 and fits this general description.

As we have said before, Halliwell is very forensically aware; he burned clothes and discarded seat covers and floor mats from his car after abducting Sian O'Callaghan to destroy forensic evidence. The carpet the Angel of the Meadows was found wrapped in had been burned, and Linda Donaldson's body had been washed down to remove fibres that could provide forensic evidence.

Linda's abduction and murder crossed force boundaries, with the abduction taking place in the Merseyside Police force area and the dumping of her body in the Greater Manchester Police force area. Again, this followed his usual patterns. Both Julie Jones and the Angel of the Meadows were found wrapped in carpet, and Maria Christina Requena's body had been put into water, which is consistent with the murders of Carol Clark and Lindsay Jo Rimer, who we suspect are other victims of Halliwell. The deposition site at Angel Meadows is just over half a mile from the Rochdale Canal, which connects the Leeds and Liverpool Canal via the Bridgwater Canal and is half a mile from the River Irwell. Both are popular fishing spots so may have been attractive to Halliwell when he planned his holidays.

Halliwell used sex workers, and he may have targeted them because they were often not missed, or not reported as missing, as we saw with Becky Godden Edwards. The sometimes-transient lifestyle of women in this profession offers a cover for someone targeting them, as people may believe the missing woman has moved away, and often the police doubt a crime has been committed as people do just decide to go missing of their own accord. Sex workers, however, are much more likely to suffer violence than a woman following a different occupation. They get into the cars of strangers and are at risk of abduction, rape and murder, at the hands of someone they choose to leave with. Consequently, there should be a greater presumption of crime in cases where sex workers suddenly and inexplicably disappear when they are working, due to these factors, instead of the assumption they have chosen to go missing.

As we see time and time again with the cases in this book, sex workers are so vulnerable to violence and especially so when working on the streets. North Yorkshire Police launched a campaign in 2018 to protect sex workers, which explicitly recognises the fact that sex workers are inherently vulnerable. The campaign aims to inform sex workers about what support is available for them, provide essential safety tips, and encourage them to report any incidents if they are a victim of crime. On their website, North Yorkshire Police state that in some sectors sex workers frequently suffer violence and other crimes committed by people presenting as clients. However, despite 80 per cent reporting to be a victim of crime over five years, the research by Universities of Leicester and Strathclyde, highlights only 23 per cent reported the crime to the police. They believe the reasons for not reporting crimes include fear that reporting and engagement with the criminal justice system would alert police to their sex work, which could lead to public identification, jeopardising anonymity or, for some, an anxiety it would lead to arrest or disruption of their business. But they wanted everyone to feel safe, saying '…we will not tolerate any crimes against those who work in the sex industry.'

Sadly, at the time these cases happened, the fact that the women were sex workers or potentially sex workers ensured that, even if the police were notified, it was unlikely the case would gain much traction. Some in the police force viewed sex workers as second-class citizens, and the lives these women lived made them the perfect target for a killer.

Becky was not reported missing for such a long time. But with Sian, instead of just a few family members reporting her missing, huge numbers of local people to Swindon (and indeed people even further afield) put a lot of pressure on the investigation, took part in searches, and got involved in appeals. This put more pressure onto Christopher Halliwell who had to move her body from his initial deposition site as the police closed in.

In response to a media enquiry asking Greater Manchester Police to confirm if Halliwell had ever been considered as a suspect in any of these cases, their Press Office stated: 'We never confirm or deny the names of suspects or where they are believed to have lived, in accordance with national policy.'

As mentioned at the beginning of this chapter, there is a fourth woman who is counted as part of the 'East Lancs Ripper' cluster in the media. We, however, do not think that her murder is linked to the others we have discussed here.

Veronica Anderson, known to friends and family as Vera, and named as such in the media, was a 38-year-old mother of two who was murdered in August 1991. She had taken a mystery phone call at just gone 10pm on the night of Saturday, 24 August 1991, which prompted her to rush out of the house. Leaving the TV on and her purse at home, she dropped her 7-year-old son off with a neighbour and asked them to watch him as she would only be gone for ten minutes, but she did not return. Just after 3am on Sunday, 25 August she was found dead in her car in a lane; she had been strangled and her throat slashed. There were no signs of a robbery or sexual assault. We believe that she was killed by someone she knew, most likely the person from the phone call she took. The *modus operandi* in Vera's case is so very different from the other three murders that whilst she is often mentioned alongside these women in the media, we do not believe it to be linked to the other three, the women we have included as potential victims of Christopher Halliwell.

Chapter 8

Trevaline Evans

Throughout this book we have looked at cases where women have been murdered and have discussed the similarities to the cases of the two known victims of Christopher Halliwell. We have also looked at cases where women have gone missing and never been found, and this chapter features exactly this type of case. Similarly to Claudia Lawrence, whose case we discussed in Chapter Four, and Linda Razzell, in Chapter Six, we believe that Trevaline was murdered, although she has never been found, and that Christopher Halliwell could be responsible for this.

Trevaline Evans was the owner of a small antiques and collectables shop in Llangollen, North Wales. The 52-year-old had been born in the town and had lived there her whole life. She was a family woman, reportedly happily married to her husband Richard, and the pair had a son, also called Richard. As well as being surrounded by her family, she was well known in the town as a kind and friendly woman who would make time to chat to her customers. She doted on her grandsons and to the outside world it seemed that all was well in her life. Trevaline and Richard lived comfortably on Market Street near to the shop, and financially they were successful. The success in their businesses gave them the opportunity to own and run a holiday bungalow in the North Wales coastal town of Rhuddlan, a part of the world they loved. The holiday bungalow was where they planned to spend their retirement. The antique shop in Llangollen, Attic Antiques, was opened every day at 9.30am and people would stop in throughout the day until Trevaline closed up at around 4pm.

Saturday, 16 June 1990 was a normal working day for Trevaline and nothing about her behaviour said otherwise. People who had visited the shop that day said she seemed her usual relaxed and happy self, and she had mentioned her plans to go out that evening. Richard was away, renovating the couple's holiday bungalow in Rhuddlan, and whilst Trevaline had spent a few days there with him the week before, she had been back in Llangollen since Wednesday the 13th to keep the shop running.

At around 12.40pm, Trevaline left the shop, and put a note in the window telling her customers that she would be 'back in two minutes'. She bought an apple and a banana from a shop on the High Street and was then spotted crossing Castle Street, but Attic Antiques did not reopen that afternoon. People who had wanted to purchase items from the bric-a-brac baskets that had been left outside the shop even put the money through the letterbox.

Richard attempted to call Trevaline a number of times that evening. Becoming more and more concerned, he rang a neighbour and asked them to go and check on his wife, but when the friend reported back that she wasn't home he asked the friend to try the shop instead. When the friend found Trevaline's car parked as normal, the shop locked up, and the hand-written 'back in two minutes' sign still hanging in the window, Richard decided to ring the police and Trevaline was reported missing.

North Wales Police immediately treated their enquiries as a murder investigation, even though there were no signs of a struggle, due to the circumstances in which Trevaline had seemingly just vanished. For example, her house keys and car keys were found inside the shop and the fact that no money was taken from her bank account after this point showed that she most likely hadn't left the area by choice. A banana skin was found in the bin inside the shop, although of course it's impossible to know whether this was from Trevaline's lunch on the 16th or a previous day. A bunch of flowers and some food items that she was planning to take home that evening were later found at the shop, along with her handbag, so it would seem that she didn't return after putting up the sign in the window.

The police took over 330 statements from the local households and checked out 700 cars to eliminate them from the investigation. The local canal, mine shafts and caves, as well as the nearby river Dee, were searched. The police had a statement from a friend who had spoken to Trevaline in the shop at approximately 12.30pm, and she was seen crossing Castle Street at 1pm so they knew the sign had been placed in the window at around 12.40pm. The sightings of Trevaline at 1pm were verified by people who knew her well. The last confirmed sighting was at 2.30pm on the same day in Market Street, once again by a reliable witness, but the police couldn't work out for sure whether she had ever returned to her shop. Locals said it was unlikely that she had because surely the first thing she would have done is remove the note.

Appeals were made in the local and national press, Richard offered a £5000 reward, and requests for witnesses to come forward were shown on the television. In one public appeal Richard stated that 'Trevaline doted on her elderly father and would not leave him behind' and no one who knew Trevaline could believe she would choose to leave of her own accord. To this day Trevaline Evans has not been found.

North Wales Police ruled out Trevaline's husband Richard as a suspect in his wife's disappearance as, not only is Rhuddlan to Llangollen a good two hour round trip by car, but multiple witness statements confirmed he was seen in and out of shops on Rhuddlan high street, and because he was back at the family home in Llangollen later. The timings of the statements given as well as the information provided by neighbours on the caravan park make it impossible for him to leave unnoticed, travel to Llangollen, kill and hide a body (presumably with some sort of argument to cause a murder), and return to Rhuddlan. Even if you give the multiple statements placing him there a bit of leeway and think the witnesses could have been out on their timings by a bit, the route to Llangollen would have taken him via the Horseshoe Pass which often takes longer to drive than expected. This stretch of road is a popular cycling route but so steep that in your car you can travel at just 8mph. This steep and long road has a severe drop on one side and no barriers, and no good overtaking spots. All it takes is to get stuck behind a cyclist and you can easily add twenty minutes to your journey.

Richard didn't fit as a potential perpetrator, not only because he couldn't have physically killed Trevaline, but the investigation into the couple's home life revealed no motive for him that the police could see.

With Richard ruled out as a suspect, detectives from North Wales Police were desperate for leads. They continued to appeal for anyone who had any information to come forward. A further review of witness statements showed that on 14 June 1990, Trevaline had been seen talking with a smartly dressed man in her shop. Again, on 15th June, she was reportedly seen walking through the town with the same man, who was wearing a smart suit and carrying a briefcase. To add to the mystery, two tourists contacted police and told them that they had seen Trevaline in a wine bar, drinking in the company of a well-dressed man. Was this the same man? He never came forward to be eliminated, although the police had done everything they could to search for him and an artist's impression was widely circulated.

After two years of investigation, appeals and searches, police still had no clue as to the whereabouts of Trevaline Evans and they announced they believed that Trevaline had been lured away somehow, possibly by someone that she knew, or at least believed she knew. They said that they did not believe the missing woman to still be alive.

In 1992, Detective Chief Inspector Colin Edwards, who was heading the continuing investigation into the disappearance, said: 'It is without doubt the strangest inquiry I have ever been involved with. How a happily married woman could vanish without trace on a sunny Saturday morning in a busy town centre is totally baffling.'

Trevaline Evans was eventually declared legally dead in 1997, although her body has not yet been found.

Detectives launched a new investigation in 2001 into Trevaline Evans' disappearance, setting up a major incident room which employed ten officers to look at every statement, phone call and piece of evidence collected at the time of the original inquiry in 1990. They really hoped that with new forensic techniques and fingerprinting technology they would be able to generate fresh leads in a bid to solve the suspicious disappearance. But, frustratingly, they were unable to find any new evidence and the inquiry was brought to a close. At this point the police also ruled that the artist's impression of the man allegedly seen with Trevaline shortly before her disappearance was no longer accurate.

The case was re-examined in 2010 on the 20th anniversary of Trevaline's disappearance, and in September 2011 it was reported that North Wales Police were looking into a possible connection between her disappearance and a convicted serial killer named Robin Ligus. Ligus is serving a life sentence for the murders of three men in 1994; all three killings took place in a six-month period only thirty miles from Trevaline's shop, and one of the victims was an antiques dealer. In January 2012, however, police ruled out any possible connection between Trevaline's disappearance and the trio of murders that occurred four years later.

Sadly, Trevaline's only child, police sergeant Richard Evans, died of a heart attack in 1999 in his late thirties and her husband, Richard, died in 2015 aged 83, both passing away without answers. In 2015, in press appeals on the 25th anniversary of his sister's disappearance, Trevaline's younger brother, Leonard Davies, spoke publicly about how the pain of her going missing has never left him. At the time, he told *The Telegraph*: 'I still think about Trevaline a lot and still miss her very much... I am forever hopeful of finding out what happened.'

What links Christopher Halliwell to this case? Llangollen is a small town in North Wales situated on the edge of the River Dee and at the foot of the Berwyn Mountain Range. It is a thriving visitor and tourist centre, with people attracted by the many beautiful and scenic walking routes it has to offer, and the River Dee is well known for the quality of its fishing. Llangollen is described by locals as internationally renowned for brown trout and grayling fishing and has good runs of salmon and sea trout throughout the season, this would be a huge draw to a keen angler.

We know that in 1994, Christopher Halliwell was living at Aughton, near Ormskirk, Lancs and that he was also working in North Wales as a window fitter. We have not been able to establish with certainty what date he started to live there, so it is possible he was living in the Merseyside/Lancashire area in 1990, in which case he could have driven the hour and a half to Llangollen to go fishing. Of course, if he was working in North Wales during the week, he could have stayed over in the weekend to go fishing. Alternatively, if he was resident in Swindon at the time, he could have driven the three hours up to Llangollen to go fishing at such a renowned angling spot.

Speaking of another of Halliwell's hobbies, the Llangollen Canal, which is popular for narrowboating, connects to the Shropshire Union Canal and then into the English Canal system. The Llangollen Basin is just five minutes' walk from the shop, and Trevaline's route from home to Attic Antiques would have taken her past the road and bridge over the River Dee that led to the Canal Basin.

Halliwell hated his mother and Sian O'Callaghan had a resemblance to her which is believed to be a contributing factor for killing her. Trevaline was older than Sian, but if you look at her photo, she bears a resemblance to her and therefore by implication to Halliwell's mother. In the video of her on the BBC's Crimewatch feature, Trevaline's hair is much darker, it is almost black, like Sian's. She had the same colour eyes and similar nose, and jawline as Sian.

No body or trace of remains of Trevaline has ever been found, suggesting a deposition site chosen carefully to avoid detection, which is consistent with Halliwell's *modus operandi.*

Trevaline's choice of business may be pertinent too. Christopher Halliwell was convicted of antique burglaries during the mid-1980s and served part of a four-year sentence, and Trevaline was in the antiques business. She was known to spend time chatting with her customers, so perhaps Halliwell is the man she was seen speaking to, posing as a potential client, the man who didn't come forward when the police appealed to him.

We suggest that Halliwell either lured her into a car with his knowledge of antiques – maybe to look at a piece he had - or took her by force, and from this point either took her to his narrowboat or to a remote area before murdering her. Trevaline's case remains open but inactive.

Chapter 9

'The Midlands Murders'

The Midlands is the central part of England, consisting of the cities of Birmingham, Coventry, Leicester, Nottingham, Stoke-on-Trent, Derby and Wolverhampton. The cases included here have been chosen because of their locality, as well as having features we suggest point to Christopher Halliwell as a suspect. Once again in this chapter we will discuss waterways and canal systems which link the abduction sites and deposition sites of the victims, as well as murders that fit Halliwell's *modus operandi*; vulnerable women murdered at night, their bodies dumped in remote areas, women strangled and stabbed, items of clothing missing and never found.

Janine Downes

Janine Helen Downes was born on 3 March 1968 in Wolverhampton. She had a sad childhood; she struggled in adulthood, dealing with spending so much of her young life in care and she turned to sex work out of desperation, trying her hardest to feed and clothe her three young children. At the time of her death, her youngest wasn't even 1-year-old and the oldest was just 3. Her dad later said he had tried to get her to stop sex work, telling her that her family would help her make ends meet another way. Janine had promised her dad that she would stop working on the streets, but she was unable to break the cycle. Janine's dad later talked about how he treasures a letter she sent him a week before her murder, in which

114

she apologised to him for not stopping sex work, fearing he was cross with her.

Reportedly a favourite with some clients because of her child-like frame, 23-year-old Janine would make herself look younger on purpose. On Friday, 1 February 1991, she was working Shakespeare Street by The Harp Inn in Wolverhampton with a 16-year-old she had introduced to sex work. The two women had met at a hostel and, after Janine introduced the younger girl to the life she led, the pair moved into what has been described as a 'seedy' flat where both of them were controlled by pimps, alongside six other girls. Both had been arrested for soliciting on a number of occasions.

Janine had briefly called into The Harp Inn with a friend, but they didn't stay for long. Janine had told friends she planned to leave for London that night, but told them that she needed to earn money for her fare first. She didn't make it to London or back home.

As the pair stood by the side of the road at about 9pm, a dark blue Ford Mondeo approached them, and the driver requested the services of Janine. It was agreed that he would pay £20 for full sex with a condom, and Janine got into the car and left with him. This was the last time she was seen alive. Janine's disappearance was reported to West Mercia Police when she failed to come home.

Janine's body had been hidden behind a hedge in a lay-by, bludgeoned to death in the early hours of Saturday, 2 February. Naked from the waist down, she had been sexually assaulted before being subjected to a frenzied attack. Owing to her size - just under five feet tall and weighing eight stone - she would have had little chance of fighting off a determined attacker. Police discovered she had been strangled with a ligature, and that she had extensive head wounds caused by a weapon with a jagged edge.

Marks on the frosty ground indicated where Janine had been dragged from a motor vehicle into the lay-by, and a pathologist estimated that her body had been dumped at some point between midnight and 4am. The wounds to her face were so horrific that the police could not be sure it was Janine until they had confirmed with her pimps that she was missing; not only an incredibly distressing scenario for the West Mercia Police detectives investigating her murder but also for her family and loved ones to learn about. When she was found, all Janine was wearing was a paisley pattern blouse, a bra and blue ankle socks. Her other clothes; white trainers, jeans, and a black shell-suit top with a yellow stripe bearing the words 'Nike International', have never been found. Are these some of the clothing items found in and around the pond at Hilldrop Lane, Ramsbury, Wiltshire?

Janine was found in a lay-by near Lambert's Restaurant on the A464 Shifnal to Wolverhampton road some five miles east of Telford and six miles north of Ironbridge and the River Severn, which links to the canal system at Stourport. She had been abducted from one police force area and dumped in another, this time from Wolverhampton in Staffordshire to the border County of Shropshire. This follows Halliwell's usual pattern; both Becky Godden-Edwards and Sian O'Callaghan were abducted in Swindon and carried into Eastleach in Gloucestershire and the White Horse Hill, Uffington, Oxfordshire areas, respectively.

There have been several suspects linked with Janine's death, including John Taylor, who was jailed for life in 2000 for the murder of 16-year-old Leeds schoolgirl Leanne Tiernan. West Mercia Police continue to investigate, but despite several arrests being made, nobody has been charged with Janine's murder.

On the 30th anniversary of Janine's murder, a fresh appeal was launched for information by West Mercia Police. Detective Inspector Lee Holehouse from the force's Major Investigation Unit, said:

> To date, despite a continuous and full investigation and several arrests being made, nobody has been charged with her murder and I desperately want to change that. I appeal to anybody with any information which may lead

to the identity of Janine's killer to get in touch in order that we can get the justice that Janine and her family deserve. Somebody somewhere knows what happened. Janine's family have lived without closure for far too long.

Dawn Shields

On Friday, 13 May 1994, Dawn Shields kissed her sleeping 11-month-old son goodbye and headed out to work on the streets of Sheffield's red light district, leaving him with her friend. After heading out in her black mini-skirt, see-through black shirt, black bra and ankle boots, Dawn was last seen getting into a cream-coloured car in the Broomhall area during the early hours of 14 May 1994. She was not seen alive again.

Dawn would usually ensure she was home in Pitsmoor, a suburb of Sheffield, by 1.30am to take over from her friend who was babysitting her son, but she did not return home and, at 7.30am the following morning, her friend called the police to report Dawn missing. After she had done this, she headed over to Dawn's mother's house with the baby. In an article from May 1997, *The People* newspaper reported how Margaret Shields immediately feared the worst. 'Dawn always came home, no matter what time. If there was anything wrong, she would phone me,' she had said.

Dawn's mum told the paper how her daughter had a happy, normal childhood, although losing her dad at the young age of 8 really hit her hard, Margaret and Dawn were close. It was only when Dawn got in with the wrong crowd as a teenager and fell for an older man that things started to go wrong for her. It transpired that the 29-year-old man was a pimp, and he soon forced the teenager into sex work, taking all her earnings and leaving her with nothing, not even allowing her to have her own bank account.

Whilst her mother tried her best to help, social services and the police were unable to support her in getting her daughter out of the clutches of the man, and even when Margaret pleaded with him, he simply laughed at her. Dawn was totally under his control. He introduced Dawn to drugs too, and she began using, losing weight dramatically, and even confided in Margaret that she wasn't just taking drugs recreationally, that they also helped with the pain when her pimp would hit her.

Dawn's life working on the streets was miserable, and she had an often-violent existence; a few months earlier she had been held at gunpoint by one of her clients who was under police surveillance. As soon as he produced the gun, the police pounced. But Dawn, incredibly shaken by the ordeal, was simply sent back out by her 'boyfriend'.

When she fell pregnant, the pimp stayed on the scene, annoyed to have lost a source of income but biding his time to get her back out working. She heartbreakingly wrote in a diary entry whilst pregnant: 'If only he could see what he has done to me. I know I'm only 18 but I dedicated everything to him. I thought he was all that mattered. But now he has gone and that has left me feeling really empty inside.' Soon after giving birth to her son, she was back out on the streets.

The only happiness she seemed to have was through her mum. Margaret's door was always open, the kettle was always on and she kept the fridge stocked with chocolate to treat her teenage daughter. Dawn was just 19 on that fateful night in 1994 when she disappeared.

Whilst she was reported missing the next day, it wasn't until a week later on 20 May 1994 that South Yorkshire police force joined with Derbyshire detectives to launch a joint murder inquiry. Derbyshire was the county where Dawn's body was found. Despite going missing in Sheffield, she had been found naked, partly buried by rocks and debris on the slopes of Mam Tor, a peak near Castleton in the Peak District. She had suffered severe head injuries and had been strangled before she was buried. Frustratingly for detectives, a week of persistent rain had effectively cleaned any forensic evidence away.

It was lucky that a National Trust warden had been test-driving a vehicle and needed to answer a call of nature and spotted her body, as cars weren't able to drive up there and the weather meant the area was not as popular with walkers as it otherwise might be. If the warden hadn't spotted her, it may have been weeks or months before she was discovered.

Once again, an offender had abducted a sex worker from one police force and county area to another. Not only were Derbyshire police working with the South Yorkshire police force who had begun their missing persons investigation, but they were also working with Midlands police on the murders of three other sex workers that year. The police believed Dawn had been killed somewhere else then dumped in her final resting place, and were unable to find her blouse, skirt or boots.

Close to where Dawn was discovered, just two miles away, is Speedwell Cavern. It is a tourist attraction for boating enthusiasts consisting of a horizontal lead miners' adit, which is a level passageway driven horizontally into the hillside that leads into to the cavern itself, a limestone cave. The adit is permanently flooded, resulting in Speedwell Cavern's interesting and locally unique feature; after descending a long staircase, the visitor makes the journey into the cave by boat. Originally, the guide propelled the boat by pushing against the walls with his hands, later the boat was legged through, and now it is powered by an electric motor. Could this have drawn Halliwell to the area?

Also en route between Sheffield, the Peak District and Mam Tor is the Derwent Reservoir and Ladybower Reservoir, the latter just nine miles from Mam Tor. It is a large, Y-shaped reservoir renowned for brown trout with large stocks and good yields and has thirteen miles of bank fishing available; perhaps a draw for a keen fisherman such as Christopher Halliwell.

Despite the two forces working together to investigate, Dawn's murder remains unsolved, no convictions have been made and her family have not yet had any closure. In 2019 Dawn's case was reopened by South Yorkshire Police's major incident review team, who were re-examining evidence for previously undetected traces of DNA with the hope that advancements in technology would help catch her killer. We suggest that the team should compare Halliwell's DNA with any found.

Sharon Harper

Sharon Harper was 21 years old and worked behind the bar at the Market Cross pub in Grantham town, North Lincolnshire, when she went missing in the early hours of 2 July 1994. She worked three nights a week at the pub, and on this particular Friday she headed off to work, leaving her 5-month-old daughter at a friend's house. With her boyfriend working nights, Sharon was planning to collect the baby after her shift. Her route home from the Market Cross public house would have taken her along Westgate, Harlaxton Road and then along Trent Road, about half an hour's walk, but she didn't make it back to collect her daughter. It was later described as a normal Friday night at work, and co-workers said Sharon had been in a good mood. As was standard, the staff stayed back for a drink together after closing the pub before heading home and Sharon, one of the last people to leave, was thought to have walked home between 12.15 and 12.20am.

Sharon's boyfriend had planned to meet her the following morning at 8am to go shopping, but when he got to her flat a light was on but she was not there. Sharon's body was found by children the following day in the Shepherd Construction car park in Earlesfield Lane, the opposite side of the street to the end of the Grantham Canal, half a mile from her home and just over a mile from work. She had been strangled and beaten before being dumped in an ornamental shrubbery.

Once again, we have a link to a major canal network, the Grantham Canal, which runs for thirty-three miles from Grantham, through eighteen locks to West Bridgford, where it joins the River Trent. Beyond Woolsthorpe the towpath is surfaced all the way to the A607 on the outskirts of Grantham. Because the waters are well stocked with Tench, Roach and Rudd it is a popular section with anglers. The Denton Reservoir was also constructed specifically to supply the canal, it is fed from springs in Denton park, and is a popular fishing location. Here anglers can fish for Tench, Carp and Bream.

Lincolnshire Police had a number of leads to follow, and over the years five people were arrested in connection with her murder, but no one was charged. Despite BBC Crimewatch appeals and reconstructions, and detectives following up on a number of leads, Sharon's murder remains unsolved.

In the course of their investigation, the police received sightings of a car said to have been parked in Shepherd Construction car park at about 3.35am on 3 July 1994, which they were interested in tracing. It would be interesting to know whether there were detailed descriptions of this car, and if so, whether this has been checked against the eighty or so registered to Halliwell we have previously mentioned. We have seen in a number of the cases covered in this book that cars and vans had been spotted around the times of the women being murdered or their bodies dumped and suggest these are cross-referenced with Halliwell's vehicle history.

Other reports stated that Sharon Harper had been seen arguing with a man who was described as being around 30 years old. Halliwell would have been in this age bracket at the time. An anonymous caller had told Lincolnshire Police on 4 July 1994 that he had seen Sharon arguing with a man and that he stopped and asked if she was alright but said that Sharon told him that she was fine and so he drove off. A taxi driver added that he had seen Sharon between 12.40am and 12.45am on Wharf Road near the roundabout, having apparently gone back towards the Market Cross pub . The taxi driver said that he saw Sharon by the phone box arguing with a man and that it had seemed as though the man had been pulling Sharon away from the phone box but that she had been trying to get into it. There was also a report that a few weeks prior to her murder, a man had seemed to follow Sharon, making her appear uncomfortable. Was this related to her murder? A friend of Sharon's told police that she had seen Sharon in the passageway at the rear of Morrison's supermarket, talking to a man on a corner and that the pair looked to be talking 'quite intensely'. She said the pair were still there when she came back out of the supermarket ten to fifteen minutes later, but that Sharon walked away from the man and towards her, stopping to chat, and it was only then that the man walked on.

She noted she thought that Sharon looked relieved to see her, but when she asked her friend who the man was, Sharon told her it didn't matter and that she didn't want to tell her. Was this potentially the man from the pub? Or was it Halliwell? Or were both the same man? We have seen previously that he was known for becoming obsessed with women, it is possible that he had become infatuated with Sharon.

During 2017, we exchanged emails with Sharon Harper's daughter, Sara, who was raised by Sharon's parents after her mum's murder. Chris explained his interest in Sharon's case, and the reasons for believing Halliwell could be responsible. Sara asked whether anyone had interviewed Halliwell or had mentioned the name Sharon Harper to see if he knew anything, but of course we were unable to help answer that for her. Sara thanked us for getting in touch and she has been vocal in the press about wanting to get answers for the mum she didn't get to know, answers to the mystery that Halliwell could potentially reveal.

Lindsay Jo Rimer

Lindsay Rimer was 13 years old and lived with her parents, two sisters and her brother in the family home in Hebden Bridge, a market town in West Yorkshire, when she went missing in the evening of 7 November 1994. She had headed out to go shopping, stopping at the Trades Club, where her mum was enjoying a night out, to get some money from her. Her mum was having a drink with a friend and asked Lindsay if she wanted to stay and have a cola with them, but Lindsay said no and continued to the Spar supermarket to buy a packet of cornflakes for her breakfast the next day. CCTV footage from the shop showed her paying for the cornflakes at 10:22pm.

When she didn't show up to her paper round the following morning, the newsagents rang her home and reported to her parents that she hadn't arrived as usual, and they then reported her as missing. West Yorkshire Police believed that she was one of the thousands of teenagers who run away every year, even though Lindsay's family and friends were adamant that the popular teenager wouldn't have done so. It is unknown as to why they didn't take this more seriously, considering her family's protestations that she would not have chosen to run away, but as The Children's Society state on their website, every year in the UK 100,000 children and young people go missing or run away from home. That is 144 children who go missing or run away each day in the UK.

Lindsay's older sister took part in a reconstruction of her walk to the shop and hundreds of local people joined the police in searches of the area around Hebden Bridge, but no trace of Lindsay was found until five months later, on 12 April 1995, when two local canal workers made the horrific discovery of her body in a lock of the canal, weighted down by a concrete boulder. The pair were a mile or so outside Hebden Bridge, towards Todmorden, where the Calder River and Rochdale Canal run only yards apart. One of them was clearing debris at the Rawdon Lock, removing tyres, bits of wood, all sorts of debris, when they found something they couldn't remove by hand, something about a foot underwater.

Using a grappling hook to lift the unknown object, they soon realised they had discovered a body and phoned the police. Being locals, they had been well aware of the missing teenager, and knew right away that they had found Lindsay. One of the pair had even known her. He said of the discovery: 'It has stayed with me, it always will.'

Within an hour of the grim find, police had removed the body. The post-mortem was carried out later that day at Royal Halifax Royal Infirmary by Home Office pathologist Professor Mike Green, the man police turned to throughout their difficult investigation into the crimes committed by Peter Sutcliffe. He concluded that Lindsay had probably been strangled. Her voice box had been flattened against the spinal column and there were also signs of congestion across the middle of the neck muscles. There were no signs of a sexual assault, however, the body had spent months in the canal and had suffered too much serious decomposition to make an accurate post-mortem report. Despite the condition of the body, the pathologist was able to determine that Lindsay had been strangled. Her voice box had been flattened against the spinal column and there were also signs of congestion across the middle of the neck muscles. Halliwell had murdered Becky Godden-Edwards in a similar fashion and Sian O'Callaghan had died from a combination of two stab wounds to the neck and head as well as compression to the neck.

The conclusions from the post mortem provided the basic foundations on which the police began their murder inquiry. It will, in due course, provide expert evidence in the prosecution of Lindsay Rimer's killer. Only the sketchiest details have been made public and many elements of the post-mortem report – especially the arrangement of Lindsay's clothing – have been deliberately withheld by the police for tactical reasons.

Lindsay's body had been weighted down with a 20lb rock which in turn was tied with a number of lengths of rope knotted together which bound her body, this configuration is very similar to that used to tie the remains of Melanie Hall and Maria Christina Requena, other suspected victims of Halliwell. In our estimation, it would be virtually impossible for Lindsay's abductor to have the rock and rope at her abduction point near the Spar Supermarket in

Crown Street and highly improbable that bound and weighted in this fashion, carried along a towpath to her deposition. The only scenario which fits is that she was abducted after leaving the shop, bundled aboard a river craft (narrowboat) where she was kept until the craft made Rawdon Lock.

The distance between Lindsay's abduction and deposition sites is over a mile westerly and against the natural flow of the canal. The canal starts at Sowerby Bridge in West Yorks and rises all the way to Summit past Todmorden, which is over four miles west of Hebden Bridge; so it would appear that she was kept on board a river craft to attain that distance.

In 2016, Lindsay's sister Juliet spoke to the press on the anniversary of her sister's body being found. She was only a baby at the time Lindsay went missing and grew up not knowing the sister she should have had, but was incredibly aware of the impact Lindsay's murder had on her loved ones. She said:

> There will always be a void. I have no memories of her of my own; everything is from photographs, stories and the media. It is heart breaking to watch your family break down every year, knowing there is nothing you can do but be there for them. Not knowing what happened is the worst part. You walk down the street and wonder, 'Was it them? Do you know something?' Getting the answers wouldn't change the hurt but it would help bring closure to us all.

At a press conference at the time, Lindsay's mother said, 'My little girl deserves justice. We live in a complete state of turmoil, not just on anniversaries but every day. I need to know what happened to my daughter. She didn't deserve to die.'

It was also revealed in 2016 that a DNA profile of Lindsay's killer had been obtained, although West Yorkshire Police did not disclose where it was from. At the time detectives revealed that they had been working with a forensic provider in Canada to generate new forensic leads, but no matches had been made. We suggest that this is compared by the police with Halliwell's DNA.

Detective Superintendent Simon Atkinson from the Homicide and Major Enquiry Team, who led the investigation, was quoted in 2016 as saying that the police have a determination to get justice and won't close the case until they do. The West Yorkshire Police investigation into Lindsay's murder has been huge; police have taken hundreds of witness statements and spoken to more than 5,000 people during their investigation. There have also been two arrests made over the years; a 63-year-old man in November 2016 and a 68-year-old man in April 2017, but frustratingly for Lindsay's family and the police there has still not been a conviction made in this murdered teenager's case.

There are some similarities between Lindsay's murder in both victimology (age group) and methodology (connection to narrowboats) to the case of Hannah Deterville, whose case we discuss in Chapter Eleven. Whilst both teenagers are younger than his two known victims, Halliwell is known to have been worried that police were investigating him over allegations involving underage girls, and his victim type was petite young women; these two streetwise teens may well have appeared older than their years.

Michaela Hague

On Bonfire Night, 5 November 2001, 25-year-old Michaela Hague watched fireworks in Sheffield with her partner and their 5-year-old son, before setting off to Corporation Street, which was in a red light district. Michaela was a heroin addict and had turned to sex work quite recently to fund her habit; she had been working the streets for about six months. Witnesses described seeing her getting into a blue, old style Ford Sierra with a roof rack sometime after 7pm, and by 8pm she had been fatally stabbed.

Michaela was discovered semi-conscious by another local sex worker in a car park at Spitalfields at around 8pm. This car park is close to Corporation Street, just a two-minute drive away, on the banks of the River Don and is known for being used by sex workers and their clients. One of the first South Yorkshire Police officers on the scene, PC Richard Twigg, wrapped Michaela in his jacket and as she bravely gasped out a description of her attacker, he wrote notes onto his hand. He then accompanied Michaela to hospital, but despite PC Twigg's efforts and those of paramedics, she died in hospital three hours later. Michaela had been stabbed nineteen times in her back and neck, the post-mortem stating this was probably while she was lying face down on the ground. Michaela had described the man who stabbed her as white, about 38 years old and clean shaven, saying he was about 6ft (1.8m) tall and he wore a blue fleece, glasses and a wedding ring. An e-fit was created and released to the media, an image of a man who bears a striking resemblance to the tall, slim, short-haired Halliwell.

Michaela's heartbroken parents Jackie and Mick Hague, from Parson Cross, only found out that Michaela had been working as a sex worker when police broke the news that she had died. Weeping at a press conference, they said their daughter was a loving child from a caring family. 'She was a lovely, beautiful daughter,' said her mother, who emotionally explained how the murder had ripped their family apart.

In the first few hours after the murder, South Yorkshire Police detectives conducted a painstaking search of the area where Michaela was attacked and sent items off for forensic examination in the hope that technology could help them identify the killer, in addition to piecing together how Michaela lived her life. It led them to identifying and investigating her regular customers and speaking to other sex workers and men known to visit Sheffield's red light district at that time. In a bid to encourage men who knew her to come forward to eliminate themselves from the investigation, detectives threatened to track them down and visit them at home. This did prompt more men to come forward who were probably worried about the potential of an embarrassing knock at their door.

As well as the description given by Michaela, South Yorkshire Police said that they managed to get some DNA evidence but had not been able to identify whose it was. Detectives who have worked on the murder investigation over the years have regularly suggested that advances in DNA could be the key to solving the case. They have stated that they have some forensic evidence stored away that they can use as and when there are advances in science, and as with other cases discussed, we believe it would be important to test this DNA evidence the police have from Michaela's murder against Halliwell's.

The car park where the attack took place no longer exists, being physically swept away when the Derek Dooley Way section of Sheffield's ring road was constructed. However, it was only a two-minute drive from where Michaela was picked up in Corporation street to the car park in Spitalfields, a distance of just 0.2 miles, crossing the River Don at Bridgehouses Bridge. Sheffield Basin with its narrowboat moorings is only a four-minute drive away, a length of 0.6 miles, and features many weirs and locks. Most of the river holds stocks of grayling, trout and chub and occasionally, salmon. Again, a place of interest perhaps for a keen fisherman or narrowboat enthusiast.

During 2011, on the tenth anniversary of the murder, Michaela's partner, Mick Holmes, urged anyone with information to come forward fearing the killer could strike again:

> There can be no bigger sin than taking a mother away
> from her child. He has caused a huge amount of damage
> to me, our son and Michaela's family … What he did
> to Michaela, something so savage, is not the kind of
> thing somebody just does once – I am convinced he has
> either done it before or will do it again, although I pray,

he doesn't so that no other family has to go through what we have. I just want him locked up – I would rest a lot easier knowing he wasn't out there able to do this again. My one fear is he will do it again.

All of the women described in this chapter were vulnerable due to their jobs or walking alone at night, making them a perfect target – in both of the cases he was convicted of, Halliwell snatched his victims at night time. He used the services of sex workers and was known to frequent red light districts, so the women discussed here may well have known him or had him visit them as a client.

The abductions or deposition sites are all close to waterways enjoyed by narrowboat enthusiasts and fishermen, hobbies we know Halliwell enjoyed. As with many other cases presented here, and as we saw with Becky and Sian's murders, items of clothing were taken and never found. We would like to suggest again that the police check Halliwell's long list of vehicles for matches to any of the cars spotted in these cases, and that the items of clothing found in the pond at Ramsbury are looked at in detail for the items missing in these cases. There is DNA evidence available that we believe the police should ensure is tested to eliminate Halliwell as a suspect.

Chapter 10

'The River Tees and Yorkshire Murders'

Within this chapter, we have highlighted four cases which we have grouped together due to locality. Middlesbrough is a large town in North Yorkshire, northern England, and sits on the southern bank of the River Tees. Darlington is located in the south of County Durham close to the River Tees, which acts as the border between Durham and Yorkshire. The two towns are twenty-five minutes' drive from one another.

The cases discussed here again feature witness statements where the suspect matches the description of Christopher Halliwell. We will discuss cases with sex workers as targets, abductions taking place late at night and cases of women who went missing and have never been found. As before, the methods of the murders discussed also follow Halliwell's known *modus operandi*, and we will explore links to waterways and canals. These are four more women for whom we want justice, four more families and communities who deserve answers.

Ann Heron

At the beginning of August 1990 there was a hot spell and, on 3 August, temperatures in the UK reached 37.1°c in some places. Like many others in the UK at the time, 44-year-old Ann Heron was enjoying the fine weather outside and was spotted by a friend sunbathing at around 3.30pm in the back garden of her home, Aeolian House.

The Herons were a reasonably wealthy couple, and their four-bedroom house was a large detached property, described as the most expensive in its postcode. Whilst the large, luxurious home was isolated, surrounded by five acres of woods and countryside and situated on the outskirts of Darlington, Co Durham, it was visible from the A67, and the friend who saw Ann was sat on the top deck of a bus as it drove past. It is assumed that Ann continued to sunbathe in her bikini at home for the rest of the afternoon.

Ann's husband, Peter Heron, returned home from work at the haulage firm GE Stiller Transport at around 5pm to discover a terrible scene, one that would stay with him for the rest of his life. On the lounge floor, in a pool of blood, was the lifeless body of Ann Heron; her throat had been cut. There were no signs of a break-in, and her radio was still playing. Her bikini bottoms were missing and were never found. Peter could see that nothing had been taken from the cottage.

Ann's daughter, Ann Marie Cockburn, planned to visit her mother that day, but was running late, and instead received a phone call informing her of her mother's murder. Tragically, a thought she could never quite get from her mind was that if she had left on time, she may have arrived just before the murder occurred. Ann's dog, Heidi, was discovered unharmed at the scene of the crime. Whilst, of course, Ann and her family are the main victims here, pets suffer too, and in this case the dog was left with emotional scars. Following the murder, Ann's daughter Ann Marie said that the dog had become extremely anxious and was scared of men she didn't know.

Ann has been described as beautiful and kind, and her daughter said: 'She was such a lovely, mild-mannered, caring lady who always thought of others before herself.'

Durham Police immediately set about appealing for witnesses, and five people reported seeing a man leaving Aeolian House, driving erratically, in a blue Ford Sierra or Austin Montego at a time established by police to be shortly after Ann's murder. He was driving so fast that he almost crashed into another vehicle. This man was described as a white man who was 'suntanned' and estimated to be in his early thirties.

Another witness came forward, stating that he had seen Ann on the afternoon of her murder, driving a vehicle with two passengers. He said that she had been driving towards her home, and that he had seen her turn into the road towards Aeolian House. This seems unlikely given that she was in the same bikini that she was found in when she was seen by her friend on the bus. It is more likely that this witness was mistaken, and Ann had been sunbathing all afternoon.

According to Home Office statistics, in 37 per cent of cases where a woman is murdered in the UK, the assailant is her husband, boyfriend or lover. So naturally, Peter Heron was a key suspect at the beginning of the case. Durham Police detectives soon discovered that he had been having an affair with a bar worker at his local golf club, and began to focus their attention on him. However, there was no evidence linking him to Ann's murder in any way and the investigation slowly wound down.

In 2005, advances in DNA testing allowed police to re-test the evidence they had recovered from the scene. At this point detectives discovered that Peter Heron's DNA was identified on the body of his wife. Given that he had discovered the body, and the crime had taken place at the family home, this was hardly a surprise. Nonetheless, in November 2005, Peter Heron was arrested for Ann Heron's murder. He was charged with murder after police located a 'tiny speck' of his DNA on Ann's body. However, all charges were later dropped following 'additional expert opinion in a key area of the prosecution's case'. The case was never taken to trial, but the reasons for this have not been declared.

Peter Heron was 55 years old with grey hair at the time of the killing and bore no resemblance to the suspect seen fleeing the scene.

Such a public arrest can, of course, taint the reputation of an innocent person forever. Whilst all charges were dismissed in the case against Peter, he still suffered the indignity of being accused in the press, along with the distress and worry the police investigation and the preparations for court would have caused him.

In 2021, Peter's daughter, Debbie Simpson, revealed that she made a complaint about the handling of her stepmother's case by Durham Police. She said the case had been 'damaging' to Peter and his family: 'In our opinion, Durham Constabulary failed to meet their own high professional standards which compromised the quality of their investigation.'

We believe the Ann Heron investigation has been derailed, to some extent, by two false lines of enquiry; firstly, the police focussing on Peter Heron as their main suspect and the witness sighting of Ann turning into the drive with two men in a car.

We have seen before how easily disrupted an investigation can be if the focus is put on the wrong clue or witness statement; a prime example of this being the weight placed on the 'Wearside Jack' letters and cassette in the middle of the hunt for Peter Sutcliffe. Instead of focussing on witness statements and descriptions, the police ignored warnings that the letters and cassette recording were hoaxes and instead put a lot of time, money and resources into investigating these as being real. The misdirection of the police at the hands of John Humble allowed the so-called 'Yorkshire Ripper' to continue attacking women for a further eighteen months before being caught. Humble actually twice phoned the police anonymously to indicate they had been hoaxed because he felt guilty for misleading the investigation, but his calls were discounted as hoaxes themselves, and he appears to have suffered with the guilt of his actions for the rest of his life.

In his book on the Halliwell investigation, Detective Superintendent Stephen Fulcher emphasises the danger of becoming inflexibly focussed on one line of enquiry: 'Before you know it you've created a whole story of your own generation... I'd seen it happen many times before.'

We believe that the prime suspect must remain the suntanned man in his early thirties seen fleeing Aeolian House in a blue Ford Sierra or Austin Montego shortly after the estimated time of death. He has never been identified but we suggest that Christopher Halliwell's car history is checked for this specific type of car, especially given Halliwell's past offences of burglary – the crime seems to suggest a break in and, as Ann's friend could see her sunbathing from the bus, it follows that others could too.

Donna Keogh

Donna Marie Keogh was born on 29 November 1980, to parents Brian and Shirley. She was the middle child of three and grew up in Middlesbrough. She was a very popular girl who loved spending time with many friends and cousins who were of a similar age to her. Donna had a keen interest in fashion, loved to do her hair and makeup, and took pride in her looks. Donna was a strong swimmer who would often go to the local pool in her spare time and loved to listen to her dad's stories and memories from his time serving in the armed forces; she was incredibly proud of him. One of her ambitions was to join the Royal Navy as a nurse, such was her love of caring for others. At the age of 16, Donna put this compassionate side into practice, working at a care home for the elderly.

In April 1998, Donna had been living at her cousin's house, which was in Middlesbrough town centre. On 18 April she headed out with a group of friends to a house party. After spending time with them through the night she left the party at about 11pm. The last time Donna was seen at the party, her friends described her outfit, saying she was wearing a sky blue backless dress and black knee-length boots. Donna was never seen alive again.

As Donna would usually keep in contact with her family, to whom she was close, it was unusual for them not to hear from her. They reported her missing when they hadn't heard from her for a while, and Cleveland Police opened a missing from home inquiry. A witness came forward to say they had seen Donna at 3am on Hartington Road, near the Shipmate pub, being forced into a red hatchback car. This car headed along Newport Road which leads to Newport Bridge and the Tees Barrage Bridge.

Donna's body has never been found, and the police soon moved from a missing person's case to investigating her disappearance as a murder. Sadly, aside from the last sighting of Donna near the Shipmate pub, there have been no leads and to this day what happened to her remains a mystery.

Although we don't like to criticise the police, in this case we believe that poor investigation hampered many clues being uncovered. The police actually came under fire for their investigation of the murder when Donna's parents ultimately made a formal complaint. The complaint included, amongst other things, that police officers had issued press statements alleging their daughter was a sex worker, although this was not so. An apology was demanded for this, which Donna's family did finally receive in 2015.

In June 2018, Cleveland Police revisited the case and conducted a search for Donna Keogh's body in wasteland in Middlesbrough, but sadly this search was unsuccessful.

Did Christopher Halliwell kill Donna Keogh? We have so little to go on, but her abduction late at night into a car fits his *modus operandi* and her missing body suggests someone who was skilled at disposing evidence.

Vicky Glass

Vicky Glass was born in September 1979 and was brought up in the Roseworth area of Stockton, attending nearby Blakestone School. In early 2000 she moved to an address in Middlesbrough, and she was living here when she was reported missing in the September of that year. She had turned to sex work to feed her heroin addiction and was described as a frequent visitor to Middlesbrough town centre for work. She was also known to leave town with lorry drivers who would pay for her services. The 5ft 3in tall woman was last seen wearing a white t-shirt, light grey trousers and white trainers, being dropped off by taxi outside the Shipmate pub in Middlesbrough town centre. It was about 4am on Sunday, 24 September 2000.

A missing person's inquiry into Vicky's disappearance became a murder investigation when, on 3 November 2000, a dog walker discovered her body in a stream, a tributary of the River Esk. She was found in a remote area of the North York Moors, near to the village of Danby, forty miles away from where she had last been seen in Middlesbrough, along the A171 Road and close to Scaling Dam Reservoir.

She was naked and the condition of her body led police to believe she had been on the windswept moor for a number of weeks. The coroner recorded an open verdict into Vicky's death. Her clothes and possessions have never been found.

After Vicky's body was discovered, police launched a massive manhunt appealing for friends and clients to come forward with any information they may have. During the hunt for the killer, hundreds of people were interviewed, and detectives took thousands of statements. In early 2001 a 39-year-old lorry driver from the Grimsby area was arrested in connection with her death but was later released without charge. Then in January 2002, a 47-year-old man was arrested but he was also released without charge.

In 2019 there was a fresh appeal launched by Cleveland Police, with Inspector Pete Carr saying:

> Vicky would have been 40 this weekend, but her life was
> cut short at such a young age and her family and friends

have been robbed of precious time with her. Someone knows what happened to Vicky, and that information will have been a weight to carry over the last two decades. Now is the time to come forward, our investigation is continuing and someone may be able to give us the last piece of the jigsaw so we solve this case and get justice for Vicky and her family.

Once again, we have a victim last seen at night, who was found close to a place popular with fishing enthusiasts. If Halliwell were to visit the area for fishing or boating, he would also have found himself close to the red light district, thus giving him the opportunity to fulfil another of his habits, utilising the services of sex workers.

Rachel Wilson

Rachel Wilson was a sex worker who solicited in Middlesbrough town centre. Like previous victims, she had turned to this line of work to pay for her drug addictions. She was last seen on 31 May 2002, caught on CCTV images walking through the town centre at around 11.30pm the night before, at 3.30am that morning and finally at 7.02am. At this point she was just half a mile away from where Vicky Glass was last seen.

Rachel was described as being 5ft 5in tall, with blue eyes and long brown hair and on the night she went missing, she was last seen wearing a cream padded jacket with a hood, a white top, three-quarter-length trousers and blue suede shoes. Rachel phoned her mother every day and was in close contact with her family despite her addictions and lifestyle. When her mother didn't hear from her, she was naturally worried and reported her missing. She told police that her daughter was not the type of woman to move away without discussing her plans with her mother and this was totally out of character fo her.

And indeed, the police were also immediately worried when their investigations highlighted that Rachel had not visited any of her usual drug dealers either.

Closure did not come soon for Rachel's family; in fact, it was not until a decade later on 27 June 2011 that her remains were discovered. A farmer, who was carrying out drainage work in a remote area of woodland, came across Rachel's naked remains in a shallow grave near to the Newham Hall Farm Estate in Coulby Newham. Whilst Coulby Newham is a housing estate that's only a fifteen-minute drive from the city centre, the Newham Hall Farm Estate specifically is a mixed farm of 460 hectares.

Experts, including forensic archaeologists, were brought to the scene, but no viable evidence could be recovered. The post-mortem was also unable to find the cause of death due to the fact that the remains had been there so long. Rachel's clothing and belongings were missing and have not been found.

Rachel was finally laid to rest in September 2012, and her funeral at Teesside Crematorium was attended by more than a hundred people.

In October 2020, 61-year-old Keith Thomas Joseph Hall, Rachel's former pimp who had been on police bail for four years, was charged with the murder of the teenager in 2002. Keith Hall was more than twenty years her senior and was older than Rachel's own mother. He was the police's prime suspect, having been the one to lead the teenager into a life of addiction. In addition to murder he was charged with living off immoral earnings but maintained his innocence and denied all the charges.

At Teesside Crown Court on Tuesday, 11 May 2021, Hall, who had initially pleaded not guilty to Rachel's murder, and had at no time admitted to being involved in Rachel's death, changed his plea to guilty at the start of his trial. The Crown Prosecution Service accepted the plea to the lesser charge of manslaughter and declined to pursue the murder charge because it would be 'very difficult' to prove intent, the judge said, and the guilty plea was accepted. He was jailed for 18-and-a-half years.

The Cleveland Police force linked Rachel's murder to the murders of Donna Keogh and Vicky Glass, and in 2018 they revealed that there would be an active cold case investigation into all three murders. The force secured Home Office funding to solve the cases of the girls, following a review of the application to the Home Office which noted poor quality investigations into the murders. The application also showed failings by the force in relation to the three women. At the time, Detective Chief Superintendent Jon Green said:

> Cleveland Police has already recognised publicly that there were shortfalls in the initial investigations and we have met with the families to discuss concerns they may have had around this issue. We repeat our pledge to all the families involved that we recognise the unimaginable torture they have endured over the years and we would state again our absolute determination to leave no stone unturned in our efforts to discover what happened to these three young women - and to seek justice for them.

All three murder cases were re-opened and a specialist team was set up to focus solely on these three cases. Whilst there has been the update of Keith Hall pleading guilty to manslaughter, we concluded, as Cleveland Police originally did, that the three cases were linked.

Refreshingly, in this case, we have been contacted by Cleveland Police and have forwarded our research around Halliwell's potential connection, but it is unclear if Halliwell has ever been considered as a suspect in this new investigation.

So, why do we think Christopher Halliwell might be responsible for these murders?

139

Halliwell was familiar with Yorkshire, and Middlesbrough and Darlington were certainly within travelling distance for him, in his movements around this area of the country. Aeolian House is five miles from Darlington (about eight minutes driving time). Going further afield, it is fifteen miles (roughly twenty-five minutes driving time) from Middlesbrough along the A67, via Middleton St George. There are also key roads linking the area to York and Scarborough – travelling along the A19 and then the A67, via Middleton St George, Aeolian House is forty-nine miles (about one hour and seven minutes driving time) from York, and sixty-two miles (roughly one hour and thirty-five minutes away by car) from Scarborough along the A171 via Middlesbrough.

Scarborough could be significant to the three Middlesbrough murders, as the route from Scarborough to Middlesbrough goes to the fishing spot at Scaling Dam, and very close to the deposition sites of Vicky Glass and Rachel Wilson at Danby and Coulby Newham. As there is no red light district in York, Middlesbrough has the closest red light district to Scarborough. Donna, Vicky and Rachel were both abducted from Middlesbrough town centre, and it has been confirmed that Halliwell was seen in Scarborough in the period covering all three murders.

Halliwell started his criminal career as a burglar, raiding isolated properties for antiques as well as car thefts. Aeolian House is exactly the sort of home he would have targeted back then, so he would have had experience with homes similar to where the Herons lived. Whilst Ann's murder is very different to the other murders described here, we suggest that Halliwell saw an opportunity to rob a home he could tell was owned by wealthy people, but was disturbed by Ann, not expecting her to be home. Or perhaps he simply saw Ann in her garden sunbathing in her bikini and chose to conduct an opportunistic attack on a woman he soon realised was home alone.

If we look at the reasons why Halliwell may have been in the area of Aeolian House when Ann Heron was murdered, two particular hobbies stand out; his love of fishing and narrowboats. As we have discussed, Halliwell was known to frequent popular leisure craft and narrowboat venues, and just one mile to the south east of Aeolian House there is a very popular fishing venue at Middleton St George Water Park. Darlington Anglers Club is based at Cleasby and has approximately nine miles of river fishing coarse fish which includes pike, bream and carp. The River Tees is known for its brown trout, grayling, salmon and coarse fish. Cleasby is five miles to the west of Aeolian House. Yorkshire has an extensive canal network, and the River Tees has excellent fishing along most of its length until the Tees Barrage. There is also excellent fishing at Scaling Dam, close to where the body of Vicky Glass was dumped at Danby and Danby is along the route from Scaling Dam to York.

Halliwell fits the description of the man seen leaving Aeolian House; he had dark hair and photographs show him tanned. If he was on holiday or working in the area in August, he may have been facially tanned from time in the open, fishing. He was 26 in August 1990, not quite early thirties, but this could be due to an error by the witnesses. The car spotted may well be one of the many registered to him in the past.

Halliwell used sex workers and may have become familiar with the centre of Middlesbrough from this interest, and the area around the Shipmates' Pub where Donna and Vicky were abducted from. We believe that this pub, now The Junction, is the epicentre of these three murders.

Halliwell was often described as well-dressed, clean, and tidy. He was also labelled as charming and persuasive. He would have no difficulty persuading any of the victims to accept a lift from him.

Two of the victims were taken either into the neighbouring force area of North Yorkshire or dumped close to its boundary, the tactic used by Christopher Halliwell in the abduction and murder of both Becky and Sian. The fact that items of clothing have not been found in all of these cases links to Halliwell's *modus operandi*. Could these personal items also be in the huge collection of women's clothing and accessories that were discovered in the pond in Ramsbury?

Ann Heron's throat was slashed. Cutting someone's throat is a ruthless, brutal and gory act, indicating a person proficient with a knife, someone who had used one to kill before. A surprising number of victims of homicidal cut-throat suffer very little bleeding apart from post-mortem drainage. If the incision is wide and deep, so that the jugular veins are cut, and especially if the victim is upright, air immediately fills the right atrium of the heart and the circulation ceases – this process is called air embolism. Halliwell had been a butcher and had no compunction about using a knife on Sian O'Callaghan in a very brutal and efficient way that killed her very quickly. This would also explain why there were no bloodstains seen on the man seen driving off from Aeolian House.

The deposition site for Rachel Wilson is very similar in description to the one Halliwell created for Becky Godden-Edwards. The deposition site for Donna Keogh has never been found, suggesting she was skilfully concealed. Perhaps Donna could be the victim in the five-foot-deep grave Halliwell mistook Becky's grave for when he made a mistake with the depth he had buried her at. Vicky Glass' body was concealed by an isolated road and remained undetected for five weeks; this is exactly the same *modus operandi* Halliwell used with Sian O'Callaghan who may well have remained undiscovered had Halliwell not taken the police to the site.

No forensic evidence of any sort was found in any of these cases, aside from the later identification of Peter Heron's DNA at his wife's murder scene. As we have already discussed, Halliwell had a small library of books on forensic science and was forensically aware. He took great pains to ensure he left no forensic evidence, so it may be that he was able to destroy any links to himself. The lack of DNA evidence could be a reflection on the police and their abilities during these investigations, or it may be due to the rural weather-beaten deposition sites of Rachel and Vicky.

Ann Heron's murder occurred just three years after Halliwell's release from HMP Dartmoor. At this time, his only reported crimes had been theft and burglaries, so he would not have been considered a suspect for murder. Now, following his murder convictions and also his conversation with his cellmate, where he discussed how many victims you need to kill to be a serial killer, it is reasonable that Halliwell should be considered a viable suspect.

Chapter 11

Hannah Deterville

In August 2019, we received information from Steve Fulcher's former personal assistant, Deborah Lucy, who wanted to inform us of something she had seen in a court transcript from the 2016 trial, that Halliwell stated he had worked in London in construction in 1998. She wanted to pass this information on as we had not looked at London as an area of interest; we hadn't been aware of Halliwell's connection to the capital. Whilst new information to us, it was not a huge surprise to learn that Halliwell had worked there. Swindon and London, whilst eighty or so miles apart, are linked by the M4 motorway and you can get from one to the other in under two-and-a-half hours by car. There is also a reliable train network linking them, with the journey by train taking under an hour. It is not unusual for people from the town to take a trip to the capital city for work or pleasure, as it is such an easy route to travel.

With so many unsolved cases from London to look into, we began exploring cases that fit Halliwell's *modus operandi* in the area from that time frame. During this research we discovered the unsolved murder of 15-year-old Hannah Deterville.

Hannah Deterville was well known locally and popular; she was on first name terms with many local shopkeepers and was described as a fun girl. Her mother was a director of the Yaa Asantewaa community centre and helped to organise floats for the Notting Hill Carnival, which Hannah attended annually. At the time of her disappearance, Hannah was a pupil at Thomas Moore School, Sloane Square,

Chelsea, where she particularly liked athletics and drama. She was in the middle of her GCSE exam studies and was due to be confirmed in the Catholic Church the following month. Her mum described her as someone who made friends easily.

After celebrating the New Year with her family, Hannah had spent the following day doing her homework, helping out with chores, and had popped to a local shop. At around 5pm she had headed home to run a bath, had done her hair, then at about 6.30pm she asked if she could go and see her friends. Mother and daughter said goodbye at around 7pm, and Hannah left the home dressed in orange jeans, a grey bomber jacket and red Reebok trainers. As it was not unusual for her to spend the night away from home, her mum wasn't particularly worried that she didn't come home that night, but the following day when she had still failed to return, she rang her friends, but no one could provide any information. At this point she decided to call the police and report her daughter missing.

The family lived at Sixth Avenue, a tree-lined street in Kensal Rise, off Harrow Road, a few minutes' walk from Ladbroke Grove and the Grand Union Canal. Whilst Mrs Deterville told police her daughter was streetwise enough not to get into a stranger's car, and that she wasn't the type to run away, the police simply assured her that most missing people return within a few days. They sent out Hannah's description to other police stations, but the Deterville family felt the police failed to take Hannah's disappearance seriously enough at first. Family and friends were the ones who went out searching, they were the ones who took the time to put up posters around West London, and by the time the police began to take statements two weeks later, many people said they didn't remember anything properly.

'It was only after two weeks that the police reckoned she was vulnerable,' said Mrs Deterville. 'She was vulnerable from the beginning. It was the third week before they sent a constable to the house but by then it was too little, too late. We had already done what needed to be done, contacting the media and putting up posters.'

Three weeks later, on 24 January, Hannah was found. A body had been discovered by someone on the night of the 23rd, and this anonymous caller rang the dedicated gay and lesbian switchboard (a helpline in the UK) and left a detailed description of a body in a copse near the golf course on Horsenden Hill in Greenford.

Horsenden Hill is a twenty-five-minute drive from Hannah's home in Sixth Avenue, along a route involving main A roads. Whilst there is public transport available, the journey would take just under an hour and includes multiple bus and tube changes.

The man that found the body and called in said: 'from the concrete post (trig point) 150m in a south easterly direction, down the hill, past shrubs then it levels out and it's by the wooded bit'. The caller has never been traced.

When they arrived, Metropolitan Police found Hannah's body covered in black plastic bags, and she was wearing the same clothes she had left home in. She had been stabbed more than twenty times in the throat, face and chest in what police described as a 'ferocious attack.' Forensic examination showed the teenager had not been sexually assaulted, nor had she been robbed of her jewellery and money. Police did not think that Hannah's murder had been committed where she was found, but that she had been transported there in a vehicle and they believed that whoever had hidden the body knew their way around the place.

The park was known to be a popular site for dog walkers and was also a lover's lane. The police appealed to locals who may have been in the area. Detective Superintendent David Niccol said: 'We are aware that the woods were used by homosexual men. We believe it is possible that her body may have been discovered by a gay man or couple.' And they found that this fitted in with the way the tip had been called in, anonymously and through this specific switchboard.

The police arrived at the home of the Deterville family at 2am, waking them. Hannah's loved ones gathered downstairs to have the horrific news broken by Detective Steve Nottingham; he told them that the police were 98 per cent sure that the body they had found was Hannah's. The following morning, after a sleepless night, Hannah's mother went to Ealing hospital to identify the body. Most of Hannah's body and face was covered to avoid distressing her relatives, and ultimately the formal confirmation of identity was made through her dental records. Finally, at this point, the police launched a massive murder inquiry, making house to house calls, interviewing school friends and people who had visited the area where Hannah was found, and also appealing on BBC Crimewatch. The investigation was called Operation Maidstone and some of the most experienced detectives in the Metropolitan Police force were assigned to the hunt for the killer.

Speaking to The Independent in January 1999, Superintendent David Niccol, who was heading Operation Maidstone at the time, said: 'We cannot find a damn motive at all. What makes someone so livid with her to stab her so many times and continue stabbing her after death?'

Detectives described the attacker as someone who was potentially heavily blood stained over the weekend of 2 January, who may have been involved in the extensive cleaning of a premises or a vehicle, and who may have confided in someone and behaved strangely in that time. Detectives believed Hannah was killed within twelve hours of being abducted and that her body was kept for many days before being dumped. The police also stated that it was their belief that at least two people would have been needed to carry the body. Whilst this is what the police concluded, it is possible that one man could carry the body of a 15-year-old girl, especially a man who is physically fit. The police certainly did not consider the possibility of the body being transported on a narrowboat, but a search using maps of nearby roads and waterways shows the area where Hannah was found is about a two or three minute drive from the Grand Union Canal.

The Metropolitan Police were convinced that Hannah's killer had been known to her and was familiar with the surrounding areas of

Harrow Road and Horsenden Hill. They said they wouldn't entirely rule out the scenario of a psychopathic 'travelling salesman' but Supt Niccol said the killer was probably someone from the world Hannah inhabited, was likely to have known or met with Hannah at some time, and may have shown anger in the past.

The Police concluded that Hannah probably accepted a lift from someone she knew and that she was killed at another location, before her body was transported to Horsenden Hill in a vehicle. The police were certain that two people would have been needed to carry the body from the nearest vehicle access point to the deposition site, as they were working to the theory she had been moved in a car.

Detectives had established that Hannah visited a shop on Harrow Road on the afternoon of her disappearance, and the shopkeeper stated they had heard Hannah arguing with a person outside of the shop. Hannah hadn't told the shopkeeper who she was arguing with, and despite making every effort to trace this man, he has not been identified.

In September 1998, after nine months of frustration, new forensic experts re-examined what evidence there was. Although five people have been arrested at various stages over the years, no one has been charged; on every occasion the family felt hopeful that this would be the resolution they longed for, but each time their hopes were dashed and so their torment continued.

During this re-examination of the evidence, the new senior investigating officer, Detective Inspector Brian Pender, made a statement stating the nine characteristics the police believed the killer had. In this he confirmed a lot of what was already known, such as how it was likely that the killer would have been familiar with the Harrow Road and Horsenden Hill areas, but also requested the public think back to the time in question. They suggested the killer may acted strangely, perhaps had destroyed his clothing on the weekend, perhaps been involved in the extensive cleaning of a vehicle or premises that may have been bloodstained, and that he may have confided in someone. They hoped to jog someone's memory, but sadly there were no new witnesses forthcoming.

Hannah's case has never been solved. The frustration for her family was felt from the beginning when the police failed to take her disappearance seriously at first. Sadly, their mistake in assuming she was a runaway led to a delay in finding the teenager, and whilst Hannah's body remained hidden, much forensic evidence was lost. The family believe that if an appeal for information for a missing child had been made on Sunday, 4 January, while memories were fresh, it would have been more likely to produce witnesses.

Following the Stephen Lawrence case five years previously, the public had little confidence in the police and, as a result, did not want to be involved with them. Stephen Lawrence was murdered in a racially motivated attack while waiting for a bus in southeast London on the evening of 22 April 1993. His case uncovered institutional racism within the Metropolitan Police force, and an investigation showed the handling of the case by the police and Crown Prosecution Service was affected by issues of race. Some members of the LGBTQ+ community also didn't trust the police, and despite progress made to improve relations in recent times this may be why the anonymous caller that discovered the body and other men who were undoubtedly in the area when the body was dumped did not come forward.

Quoted in the *Independent on Sunday*, Hannah's mother said that several people had suggested possible motives but refused to speak to police, telling the paper: 'It's like there is a taboo with the police, as much as these people would like to help, they feel they cannot be involved.' She continued to appeal for people to put aside their mistrust and help the police. 'I want the police to get this killer,' she said. 'He or she might do this again.'

Because Hannah was believed to be streetwise and would not get into a car with a stranger, along with the fact that they had decided one man couldn't carry her body, the police focussed exclusively on the theory that the crime was committed by two or more local men that

Hannah knew. The investigation did not consider the possibility that it was an acquaintance from outside the area, or a charming stranger.

Speaking in 1999, Detective Inspector Pender was quoted as saying: 'Both myself and my team of officers are committed to seeking justice for young Hannah and trying to bring a degree of comfort to June and her family. This is probably the most horrific murder investigation I have been involved in.'

Whilst we have no doubt this was true, we feel that the initial police response hampered the effectiveness of the investigation. Something that was exacerbated by the public's mistrust in the police force at the time.

Where does Christopher Halliwell fit into this? Well, as previously mentioned, Halliwell is known to have been in London in 1998. Hannah's home is about five minutes' walk from the Grand Union Canal. The deposition site of Hannah's body is not far from the Horsenden Farm moorings on the Grand Union Canal which runs from the junction with the Regent's Canal at Little Venice, then through the suburbs of West London until it joins with the River Thames at Richmond. Halliwell knew the Kennet and Avon Canal very well, which joins the River Thames at Reading and can be navigated through to the Grand Union Canal in Paddington, where Hannah was abducted, and her body was deposited. The Grand Union Canal flows on to the Oxford Canal and is very close to the deposition site for Eila Karjalainen, another murder that Halliwell may be guilty of.

Hannah was abducted in the hours of darkness into a car, yet there were no witnesses who came forward to say they had seen a struggle. This is a similar method of abduction that Halliwell used to murder Becky Godden-Edwards and Sian O'Callaghan. The implication of this is that Hannah was persuaded to get into a car by someone she knew. There is, of course, the possibility she believed her abductor to be a taxi driver and therefore trustworthy. As a well-spoken, well-dressed, charming man and a persuasive speaker, Halliwell would have had no difficulty in persuading a girl to get into his car, being amiable and unassuming when offering her a lift.

Hannah was murdered with a knife. Halliwell had been a butcher and knew how to use a knife, he had stabbed Sian O' Callaghan twice in the neck and head, so the method of her murder is consistent with his *modus operandi*. He was a very strong and fit construction worker and would have had no difficulty lifting a body and transporting it on foot.

This is what we suspect happened on that fateful night; we believe Halliwell may have had access to a narrowboat, as well as his car, whilst living in London. We also believe that alongside his groundwork, he may have been moonlighting as a mini cab driver. Halliwell could have met Hannah locally previously, or he may have simply taken his chance on seeing her walking in the dark. He was a persuasive man and we theorise that he offered Hannah a lift on a cold dark January evening. Perhaps he had offered her the chance to look at his narrowboat. We believe that after this, he murdered her and it was at this point that he then took her body to the deposition site. By now it was in the early hours of the Sunday morning. Halliwell specialised in concealing his victims and he moved Sian Callaghan's body from where he had killed her to Uffington for burial. It is possible that he intended to return to move Hannah's body, or that he was planning to head back to dig a grave to conceal the body, but in the end he did not. Perhaps this was because he was not expecting the amount of activity on Horsenden Hill, maybe he was disturbed, or perhaps he had to leave the area and expected Hannah to be found sooner.

Chapter 12

'The Bath Rapist'

The so-called 'Bath Rapist' is a serial sex offender who is the subject of Britain's longest–running serial rape investigation, codenamed Operation Eagle. Suspected of committing at least seventeen attacks on women in the city of Bath, Somerset, between 1991 and 1997, his case remains unsolved. Detective Inspector Paul James of Avon and Somerset Constabulary, who led Operation Eagle, has been quoted as saying it was 'one of the most complicated and protracted investigations' that the force had ever undertaken.

This offender is sometimes called the Batman Rapist in the media, nicknamed as such after leaving a baseball cap bearing a logo from the Batman franchise at the scene of one attack. He was also called the Bath Riddler Rapist in the press, as the police believed the two attacks that occurred the evening after a BBC Crimewatch appeal was aired were made to taunt them.

Brent E. Turvey is the director at the Forensic Criminology Institute, is court qualified in multiple areas of forensic expertise and is the author of multiple forensic textbooks. He specialises in forensic science, crime reconstruction, forensic criminology, and criminal profiling. In his book *Criminal Profiling: 2012,* he discusses links between serial rape and serial homicide behaviours, stating his belief that these two should be given the same level of priority by investigators.

He explains that the act of homicide is in itself not a motive, rather, it is a behaviour that expresses an offender need. A related series of homicides can easily contain sexual aspects and motives that are expressed by sexualised behaviour. He goes on to explain that in his view the act of rape is also not a motive in itself. It is a behaviour that can express other offender needs beyond those of pure sexual gratification, such as control. He also states his belief that rape or sexual assault cases that involve offenders using any amount of force can easily become homicides given the right set of circumstances:

> That is to say, just because a series of rapes or homicides have been identified, it does not mean that the offender should be pigeonholed as a serial rapist or a serial murderer. Certainly, we can refer to an offender that way and be accurate, so long as we bear in mind that they can be other things as well.

Whilst Halliwell had no convictions for sexual or violent offences prior to his conviction for Sian's murder, we believe there is the potential that he is responsible for these crimes. It is not a huge stretch of the imagination to believe Halliwell, a controlling and manipulative man, could also be a rapist. Our research into cases that we believed bore the hallmarks of Halliwell's *modus operandi* led us to this with a simple 'gut feeling' we felt should not be ignored, and indeed, once we began looking at this series of attacks, we felt encouraged that we were on the right track. Not only did Halliwell commit sexually motivated murders, but his obsession with sex, power and violence lead us to believe he could be responsible here as well.

The first attack attributed to the Bath Rapist took place in May 1991. It was early evening in Coronation Avenue, and on returning home a woman was parking her car in the car park when she was abducted at knifepoint. Her attacker forced her into her own car and took her on a twenty-five-minute drive to Combe Hay, a rural village south of Bath, where he raped her. After the attack, he drove her back to her home.

A few months later in October 1991, an 18-year-old woman was walking up Bathwick Hill, an upmarket residential district on the Eastern bank of the River Avon. A popular hilly walking trail with city views known as the Bath Skyline begins here by the grand houses. She was dragged into a nearby field by her assailant and was raped.

In November 1994, a woman had a lucky escape in Bathwick, reporting that she had been aware of a man following her on her way back to her car. She gave a description of a man of medium build with dark hair, saying he was scruffy and somehow didn't look normal and she stated that he turned his head away so she couldn't see his face. She managed to escape after slipping in front of a lorry and getting into her car before driving away.

Only a few days after that narrow escape, another woman was approached in the Bathwick area. As she parked her car outside her home, a man sprinted toward her threatening her with an eight-inch knife. He ordered her into her car and drove her two miles east to Claverton, a small village close to the University of Bath. There he bound and blindfolded the woman and raped her in a lay-by before driving her home and fleeing on foot. We believe this shows he had parked up, waited to spot a target and then, after the attack, ran back to his waiting car. The attacker was described as being about 30 years of age and 5ft 7in with medium build and dark hair. The police reported that they believed that the victim had been stalked prior to the attack, and that the rapist would have had extensive knowledge of the lanes near the University.

In June 1996, a woman was left requiring plastic surgery for injuries suffered at the hands of the rapist. She had been grabbed from behind in Ham Garden car park in Bath's city centre by a man who put a knife to her throat and tried to bundle her into her car, but she fought back and in the struggle, he slashed her wrist tendons. He ran off, and the woman was rushed to Bath United Hospital. The woman later said that her attacker said that he would slit her throat and she feared that she was going to be murdered.

Just hours later Melanie Hall, who had gone to Cadillacs nightclub, disappeared. As discussed in Chapter Five, she was never seen alive again; we would suggest there is the possibility here that this was the same man, who left the scene of the initial attack bitter, disappointed and enraged by his failures.

In September 1996, a 19-year-old was snatched from her car following a night out with friends. This is the only attack attributed to the Bath Rapist that falls out of his usual pattern, as she was abducted in Kingswood, on the outskirts of Bristol, North East of Bath. Her attacker drove her out to a copse just under ten minutes away where he blindfolded her before raping her.

Weeks later, in October 1996, a woman reported that she had fought off a man who had attempted to get into her car in the Bathwick area. She managed to lock the car doors and drove off, realising later just what a lucky escape she had; that same evening just four miles away, a woman was grabbed by a man, dragged into an alleyway and raped at knifepoint.

In 1997 there were three attempted abductions that were reported later by women who realised they had fled the rapist. They were not reported at the time, but the women were prompted to come forward thanks to the police appeals. In the January there was a woman who fled an abduction in Widcombe, and two hours later another woman evaded a man who attempted to grab her in Oldfield Park, less than three miles away. There was also an attempted abduction in Bathwick that February, but again the woman managed to escape.

In the summer of 1998, a woman was kidnapped from her car in Beckford Gardens, close to the Kennet and Avon canal, before she was raped. She was left so traumatised that she didn't report the crime to the police until the following year when other attacks took place.

In January 1999, whilst parked at a junction in Bathwick, a man forced his way into a woman's car, ordering her to move over into the passenger seat. She managed to get out and fled, screaming, and the attacker ran away. Just fifteen minutes later a woman was abducted as she parked her car in Widcombe. Her attacker drove them to a village three miles south of Bath called Monkton Combe where he pulled off the main road onto an isolated track and raped the woman. He then drove her back to the spot he had abducted her from, and once again fled on foot.

The attacks generally took place in the winter months at darker times of the day, and the rapes usually occurred in secluded areas on the outskirts of the city. Often the Bath Rapist would force his victims to remove their underwear but replace their tights before the rape, and with one victim he forced her to put on a pair of tights he had brought with him. The rapist usually used a knife to threaten his victims.

The crimes of the man named as the Bath Rapist were highlighted on the BBC's Crimewatch programme on 25 January 2000. The next day there were two additional rapes reported in the Bathwick area that had taken place the night before, when the Crimewatch episode aired. Avon and Somerset Police later stated they felt these attacks were a taunt, saying they believed he specifically chose to attempt to attack women on the evening after the programme aired.

There was also an attempted abduction of a woman from her car in May 2000 that the police have attributed to the Bath Rapist that is being investigated as part of Operation Eagle. A number of women reported being attacked by the Bath Rapist over the years and came forward after seeing BBC Crimewatch appeals, including a woman who said she had been attacked in 1993.

Nobody was arrested following the BBC Crimewatch broadcast, although there were a number of leads phoned in as a result. The number of attacks slowed down, and it appeared the Bath Rapist had stopped, maybe he had been arrested for another crime and was incarcerated, perhaps he had died.

There has been a lot of discussion and theory around the reasons for the inactivity of the Bath Rapist; often there would be a cluster of attacks and then nothing for a number of months. At one point it appeared there had been no attacks in a three-year gap between

October 1991 and November 1994, followed by a further two years of apparent inactivity between 1994 and 1996. However, when the case was highlighted and renewed appeals were made, some women felt more able to come forward about attacks they had previously been too scared to report, including the woman who said she had been attacked in 1993. The police suspect there have been other attacks during the lulls in activity; perhaps there were attacks that occurred which have not been reported, or women who were able to flee a would-be attack, unaware of their lucky escape.

One theory is that the Bath Rapist was in prison during the periods of inactivity or that he had to work abroad or in another part of the country. Another theory was that he was a serving member of the armed forces. The police also suggested that the Bath Rapist was between relationships during the spates of attacks; they intimated that during these times without a steady partner he was sexually frustrated and that when he was in a relationship, he had no need to attack women.

In January 2001, Avon and Somerset Police undertook a large-scale operation taking DNA samples from around two thousand men whose names came up in their investigations, as there had been advances in DNA technology that were newly available to them. These DNA samples were compared to a DNA profile that had been obtained by the Bath Rapist. The process they used is LCN DNA which is Low Copy Number DNA profiling, a technique that has been in use since 1999 and allows a profile to be produced from only a few cells. This means it could be created from just a few cells of skin or sweat left from a fingerprint.

The police have stated that their suspect has a detailed geographical knowledge of Bath, and that they believe him to be:

- A white male;
- Of slim or medium build;
- Aged between 30 and 50;

- Someone who knows the Bath area well, and has some connection with Bristol, particularly the Kingswood area, and can drive a car;
- Someone who has a tights fetish – he would get his sexual partner to wear tights which he may rip during intercourse;
- Someone who sometimes wears a baseball cap;
- Frequently absent from home during the evening and early hours of the morning.

Naturally Halliwell is unlikely to have been on anyone's radar for such crimes in 2001 when samples were taken, nor was he living in the Bath area, but we would propose his DNA is compared to this sample by Operation Eagle due to a number of factors which, whilst circumstantial, point to a potential suspect.

We would suggest that Halliwell fits the profile of this attacker, not just due to the age range and physical description, with witnesses reporting that the Bath Rapist was clean shaven, around 5ft 9in tall, had piercing blue eyes and a scar running underneath his bottom lip (it is clear from photographs that Halliwell has a thin scar running underneath his bottom lip) but also because he had the means, opportunity and physical strength to commit the crimes.

The police said that due to the attacks usually being between 6pm and 8pm, or between 1am and 3am, they may tie into the perpetrator's work hours. Due to Halliwell's job as a taxi driver, absences from the home during the evening and night would not arouse suspicion for him, be that from a partner or neighbours. Unlike most other people, returning late at night or being away from the home for a length of time would have been normal. Avon and Somerset Police also said they thought the Bath Rapist could have had convictions for car crime because of the ease with which he broke into vehicles, which again fits with Halliwell and his criminal past.

With the two murders Halliwell has been convicted of, he drove his victims to remote locations away from the abduction sites, late at night, and both crimes took place in the darker colder months of the year; as with the majority of the rapes in this series.

After raping his victim, the Bath Rapist would drive her car back to the area where he abducted her from, and then he would flee on foot. This suggests to us that he had a way of escape from this point, one which would therefore allow him to disappear quickly. As well as the more obvious theory of the rapist having a car nearby, which of course Halliwell would have had access to, this could suggest the use of a narrowboat moored nearby. Most of the abductions were within two hundred metres of the River Avon and the Avon and Kennett Canal, waterways well known to Halliwell.

Whilst we cannot be sure that the attacks attributed to the Bath Rapist were all carried out by the same person, the police suspect that they are linked and have grouped them as such as part of Operation Eagle. There is a lot of uncertainty in this case, due to the random nature of the attacks and the fact that there have been breaks in between, which makes it difficult to investigate, but for all the reasons we have stated above, we believe Halliwell should be looked at further by the police.

The idea that as well as being a murderer, Halliwell could well have been a prolific sexual attacker raises the terrifying possibility that all over the county, over the years there could be numerous unsolved rapes for which he was responsible.

In Conclusion

Within this book we have presented a number of cases that we believe Christopher Halliwell could be responsible for. Whilst this depraved killer will never be released from prison and is therefore no longer a risk to society, this doesn't stop us from wanting to find answers. We have one reason for writing this book: we want to get some closure for the families who love these women, and some justice for the women themselves.

There are so many things that suggest Halliwell is a serial killer who could be responsible for some of, if not all the murders and disappearances included in these pages. There are many aspects of the cases included that link all these cases together, and so many ways that the women themselves were linked.

- It is statistically unusual to see a killer begin so late in life. Whilst it is not impossible, it is unlikely for someone to commit a murder such as Becky's in their late 30s, especially without any form of escalation to take them to that point.
- In general, such cases occur 'in the heat of the moment' and are therefore less easily covered up or kept secret for so long. It is also incredibly rare to see someone commit a murder, get away with it for so long, and commit another similar murder eight years later with no victims between.
- Furthermore, Halliwell went to great lengths to conceal Becky's body, and in fact did such a good job that she was not

160

discovered until he took the police to the site where she had been buried. If this was just, as he described, loss of control in the heat of the moment, it seems incredibly unlikely that he would be able to think so clearly as to get rid of the evidence of the crime, but also that he would be able to keep such a dark secret to himself for so long. There is also the question of what he did with her head, as she was found without her skull and Halliwell refused to answer questions about what he had done with this. This is not the action of a person who has simply lashed out and gone too far, this shows a far darker quality.

- With his collection of books on forensics, Halliwell was able to use the skills he had learned to try and get away with Sian's murder. It was only through painstaking police work and a chance sighting by an ANPR camera that his car was flagged as relevant to the investigation so fast. The fact that he returned to Sian's body four times is hugely worrying to us, although he was adamant in his declarations to the police that they hadn't 'had sex'. His actions suggest to us that he had not simply acted in the heat of the moment, and that his defence that she had attacked him is nonsense.

- His comments during his first prison stretch about serial killers, along with discussions around how it feels to kill someone and his demand of the police that they never ask him about any crimes again if he told them what happened to Becky suggest that he is responsible for more than the two crimes for which he is incarcerated.

- From the sixty items of clothing and accessories the police found in a secluded pond where Halliwell liked to fish, it seems extremely unlikely that only two of these items (the ones linked to his proven victims) were left by him. Who did the other pieces belong to?

- He was also unable to explain the presence of other women's items in his home when it was searched by the police; we believe that as with many serial killers, Halliwell had a penchant for keeping trophies; taking items to feel powerful, perhaps the taking of items became a part of his *modus operandi*, his 'signature'.

- Items of clothing or accessories were missing when most of the women mentioned were found, and these items have not been recovered since. Are they amongst those fifty-eight recovered items?

- Most of the cases discussed in this book crossed police force and divisional boundaries; the victims were abducted in one area, then conveyed a distance to their deposition site.

- In many cases the events took place near to waterways and routes popular for fishing and narrowboating. We have mentioned numerous times that these were hobbies Halliwell enjoyed, and that the routes are likely to be ones he was aware of or at least drawn to in a tourist capacity. Bodies left in water are much harder to identify as forensic evidence can easily be washed away or destroyed, making water an ideal deposition site for a killer.

- A number of the women were not found for weeks, or even years after they went missing, meaning they were disposed of by someone who knew what he was looking for in a deposition site. Vicky Glass was not found for five weeks, and it took months before Shelley Morgan and Eila Karjalainen's bodies were discovered. Melanie Hall was not found for years. Some of the women were found in areas that would have usually been totally secluded, discovered by complete chance and luck, someone simply stopping at the side of the road to answer the call of nature for example. Some women, including Claudia Lawrence and Trevaline Evans, remain to be found. We know that Halliwell was skilled at hiding bodies from both of his convictions, and therefore believe he would be able to do the same time and time again.

- Some of the victims suffered dismemberment and/or mutilation after death, as with Becky Godden-Edwards. There had been attempts made to remove Linda Donaldson's head from her torso, and Ann Heron was killed in a manner suggesting someone who knew how to use a knife. Halliwell, through his work history and hobbies, had butchering skills and knew how to gut a fish.

- In each case we have seen descriptions of different vehicles from witnesses, with police stating that the assailant they were hunting would have needed transport to commit the crime. Halliwell not only had a job that afforded him the opportunities to travel all over, but also had a huge selection of vehicles registered to him throughout his adult life, meaning he could have had access to each of the cars involved. Two key examples here are the CCTV footage that showed a silver Ford Focus hatchback car driving along Claudia Lawrence's street, and the maroon-coloured Ford Granada Mark Two seen parked at the entrance to the field where Linda Donaldson was discovered.

- Halliwell also matches descriptions given in many of the cases of men who witnesses spotted either near to the scene of the crime, with the victim, or in the vicinity in the days or weeks prior to the attacks. As a strong and fit man, he would have had little difficulty overpowering these women, even women who were described as being streetwise, but he was also a charismatic man who would have been able to charm the women as well. We have seen throughout these cases that Halliwell is known to have had links to the areas in which they occurred, meaning he would have a good local knowledge of where the bodies of potential victims would remain undiscovered. We also know that he was familiar with some of the red light districts mentioned.

- The women whose cases we have discussed in this book were all vulnerable in some way at the time of their murder or disappearance. Some from walking alone, like Claudia Lawrence and Sharon Harper, or even alone in their own home as with Ann Heron. Some were at a disadvantage due to their slight stature, some due to their age – two of the cases in this book, Lindsay Rimer and Hannah Deterville, feature teenage girls at their centre. Some women were vulnerable due to alcohol consumption, some due to their lifestyle or addictions (like Linda Donaldson and Vicky Glass), and many of them due to their choice of profession, like Sally Ann John and Linda Guest.

- Sex workers are constantly putting themselves into situations with strangers or men they do not know well and are statistically unlikely to report attacks they suffer for fear of being reprimanded. They are also less likely to be reported by anyone when they go missing, and have been subject to prejudices held by the police within investigations (see the Yorkshire Ripper investigation). Similarly the media and public have often been unsympathetic to such victims too, making it less likely for witnesses to go to the police. Halliwell was known for using the services of sex workers, but he was also able to get to know them through his work as a taxi driver. Becky's murder proved that he knew these women were vulnerable to such crimes.

We suggest that Halliwell's known addresses and job history should be matched by the police to the dates and times of the cases we have discussed, at least to eliminate him from the enquiries. The police should also look into the list of registered vehicles Halliwell had access to over his life, and we would hope that images or at least descriptions of the sixty items of clothing found in the pond in Ramsbury, as well as the twelve pencil sketches, should be made public for people to check through.

During our investigation and research for this book, we put forward a Freedom of Information request, asking: 'Could you please place the twelve pencil sketches drawn by convicted killer Christopher Halliwell, seized in 2011, into the public domain in order that the locations of these can be identified as probable deposition sites of missing female victims, and progress other unsolved murders'. The whole point of requesting that these pencil sketches be placed into the public domain is to provide the opportunity for someone to identify their location, meaning resources could then be focussed to identify a possible missing victim and try to locate the burial site. We had a frustrating but not unexpected response: a refusal.

Wiltshire Police's response was that, whilst they do hold the sketches, they will not release them to the public domain as they feel to do so could be highly prejudicial to any ongoing or future investigations. Whilst they conceded that the public has a right to know how an investigation is being progressed, Wiltshire Police continued to say that the release of such evidence could cause too much distress for Halliwell's loved ones, as well as the families of potential other victims. They did agree that the disclosure may lead to a more informed public debate and could have the added benefit of the community providing increased intelligence to the police in ongoing on future investigations, which is exactly what we would hope for, but ultimately their decision was that:

> Whilst there is a public interest in the transparency of policing operations and investigations and providing assurance that the police service is appropriately and effectively protecting the public from criminals, there is a very strong public interest in safeguarding both the remaining family and friends of the victims and ongoing investigations into any possible additional offences and this will only be overridden in exceptional circumstances. In this instance, the public interest firmly lies in favour of non-disclosure of the information requested.

Quite frankly, we feel this is nonsense. With the research opportunities offered by the internet, to not share information on unsolved crimes makes no sense to us. We do not understand how releasing the sketches could possibly prejudice an enquiry; surely their release would put an end to unjustified speculation, whilst opening up avenues for investigation. As such we have appealed this rejection through the official FOI channels and await their response.

In April 2020, retired detective Mike Rees, backed by Steve Fulcher, pledged that if he was elected Wiltshire Police and crime commissioner, he would plan to launch a new investigation into Halliwell. Mike Rees, who retired from Wiltshire Police as a detective inspector in 2014 and was involved in the search for victim Becky Godden-Edwards' remains, said to the press:

> It has long been suspected that there are potentially more victims. The Wiltshire public and in fact the UK public need to be satisfied that all lines of inquiry have been exhausted. From my personal knowledge of the case, I don't believe this to be the case. Wiltshire Police is one of the most poorly funded in the country and I suspect this is one of the reasons this has not been pursued vigorously. If elected, I intend to speak with and encourage the Chief Constable to re-visit this matter and will support him by seeking extra funding, if required, allowing us to exhaust every avenue to find out if there are other victims of this killer. There could be other families out there still waiting for news on their missing loved ones.

Steve Fulcher agreed with this pledge and said that there is a clear indication of other victims, and that it is a matter of justice that the crimes attributable to Halliwell are 'thoroughly and vigorously pursued' for the next of kin of the other potential victims. In the same report, Karen Edwards was quoted as saying, 'Becky had her life taken in the cruellest of ways. There are lots of things you can forgive but I will never, ever forgive Halliwell for what he did not just to Becky but to Sian and, I still believe, many others despite what Wiltshire Police will say.' There was also a quote included by a spokesperson from Wiltshire Police who stated, 'We continue to keep an open mind in relation to any further offences that Christopher Halliwell may have committed and will follow the evidence wherever that may take us.'

We will be interested to see the outcome of this, and hope that this investigation finally brings about some answers and some closure.

Throughout our investigations, we have seen a reluctance from the police to engage with us. We have faced numerous difficulties getting answers from Freedom of Information requests, and time and time again had no response to our questions or suggestions. The police should be more interested in information brought to them by so called 'armchair detectives' rather than dismissing it altogether, especially as we see more and more cases being solved by the public. Luka Magnotta was tracked down by online sleuths, for example, and the investigation into the disappearance of Lynette Dawson on the podcast *Teacher's Pet* led to new evidence being unearthed for the trial. Why not take advantage of people who have more time and opportunity to make these links and connections if closing these cold cases is not possible because of a lack of funding or resources?

In our case, we are not simply 'armchair detectives'; one of the authors, Chris, was employed in the police service for 28 years and spent the greater part of his paid time employed in the gathering of intelligence, recognising those committing specific crimes for targeting by regional crime squads and crime pattern analysis to a national level. We feel the police should think about listening to the members of the public who have excellent research skills like Chris.

One of the women named here within these chapters could be buried in the grave Halliwell seemingly mistakenly described when he told the police Becky Godden-Edwards was buried five feet down. The women in these cases could be who Halliwell was referencing when he discussed that the police were investigating him for eight murders when they were only aware of two. The clothing items that have never been recovered may be a part of the stash from the pond in the Hilldrop Lane area in Ramsbury; these items could be returned to the loved ones of women who are no longer here. There are numerous families who could finally learn the truth about what happened to the mother, daughter, or sister they lost; a loss we are sure they feel just as deeply today.

We totally understand when the police keep information about cases out of the media, if it is something that could jeopardise an ongoing investigation, but throughout our research we have come up against a wall of silence and what feels like a lack of enthusiasm to investigate further.

In 2021, whilst we were writing this book, there was excavation work taking place at an address in Gloucester, part of the search for a potential victim of Fred and Rose West. Mary Bastholm was last seen on 6 January 1968 waiting for a bus, wearing a blue jacket, blue and white dress and carrying a blue bag, and it is believed she was offered a lift by the serial killer Fred West. Gloucestershire Police reignited their searches after receiving 'possible evidence' from a TV production crew making a documentary about Fred West for ITV. The police began excavating the Clean Plate café in Gloucester after a blue piece of material was found. Police were approached by the ITV documentary crew who informed detectives that through ground penetrating radar and the use of body recovery dogs, they had found a void within the ground of the basement, in and around where the toilet cubicles were. They had drilled a hole into that void and the dogs indicated that there may be something of interest within the void.

However, following their excavation, Gloucestershire police confirmed that they had not found any remains, or indeed anything of interest to further their investigation.

This is a great example of why the police should be encouraging the public to utilise the resources available to them, allowing the police to step in once they have some further evidence to validate an additional search or an additional investigation. Without this information from the television crew, we think it is highly unlikely the police would have begun this search, a search that had the potential to bring closure for Mary's family. Whilst she was not found at the Clean Plate café, the family of Mary Bastholm have expressed sadness that her remains have not been found, saying they won't give up and that they still hope that the mystery of what happened to her will one day be solved. This is what we want for the women named in these pages, and their loved ones.

The police don't have all the answers, and we cannot expect them to. So, this is why they need to be more transparent when they have information that is not required to be kept out of the public eye. We don't expect them to respond to every email or phone call they receive, but we cannot understand why they do not release information that could be useful. We would like to see, for example, a list or photographs of the items found at the Hilldrop Lane pond area, as well as a simplified list of the vehicles Halliwell had at his disposal, so that 'armchair detectives' can delve deeper into their investigations.

There are a number of ways in which the police could open up and be more honest with the public about the evidence they have available to them, after all we are all on the same page; we all want the cases to be solved, we all want the missing women to be found and allowed a proper burial, we all want closure for the families.

Appendix I: Table of Victims

Table 2. Modus Operandi of Crimes Potentially Attributable to Christopher Halliwell

Name of victim and year of disappearance or murder, when known	Halliwell alleged to have known Victim	Man fitting Halliwell's description seen at some point	Halliwell alleged to be obsessive about the victim	Slim or medium build	Age at death or disappearance	Enticed or forced into vehicle	Picked up from outside a nightclub or pub	Abducted late at night	Abducted early in the morning	Motive believed to be sexual*	Abduction point known to Halliwell from residence or work	Abduction point may be known to Halliwell from residence, work or visiting relatives	Canals, waterways and fishing places close to the abduction points Halliwell may have used, or is known to have used	Body not found	Body nude or semi-nude	Bindings used
1	2	3	4	5	6	7	8	9	10	11	12	13	14	15	16	17
1. Angel Meadows body				•	18/35	U/K	U/K	U/K	U/K	•			Abduction point unknown		•	
2. Eila Karjalainen				•	23	HH		U/K	U/K	•	•		Abduction point unknown		•	
3. Shelley Morgan					34	U/K		U/K	U/K	•	•		Kennet and Avon Canal		•	
4. Jacky Waines AKA Linda Guest																
5. Linda Donaldson				•	32	P		•		•	•		Leeds and Liverpool Canal		•	
6. Trevaline Evans		•											R Dee, Llangollen Canal	•		
7. Ann Heron		•		•	44	KIS		N/A	N/A	•			R Tees, R Skerne, Middleton St George		•	
8. Maria Christina Requena				•	26	P		U/K	U/K	•	•		Rochdale Canal		•	
9. Janine Downes				•	22	P			•	•			Saffordshire and Worcestershire Canal, Shropshire Union Canal		•	
10. Carol Clark				•	32	P		U/K	U/K	•	•		Kennet and Avon Canal		•	
11. Dawn Shields				U/K	19	P		U/K	U/K	•			Sheffield and Tinsley Canal		•	
12. Sandra Brewin*1				U/K	21			U/K	U/K	U/K	•					
13. Sharon Harper		•		•	21				•	•			R Witham, Grantham Canal			
14. Julie Finley		•		•	23	P			•	•			Leeds and Liverpool Canal		•	
15. Lindsay Jo Rimer				•	13			•					Rochdale Canal		N/R	•
16. Sally Ann John*1	•		•	•	23	P				U/K	•					
17. Melanie Hall*1				•	25		•	•		•	•		Kennet and Avon Canal		•	•
19. Helen Sage				U/K	22	P		•		U/K			Rochdale Canal, River Irwell			
20. Hannah Deterville			?	•	15	•		•					Grand Union Canal			
21. Donna Keogh				•	17		•	•		U/K			R Tees to Tees Barage		•	
22. Julie Jones				•	32	P		•		•			Rochdale Canal, River Irwell		•	
23. Vicky Glass				•	21	P		•		•			R Tees to Tees Barage		•	
24. Michaela Hague				•	25	P		•					Shefield and Tinsley Canal		•	
25. Linda Razell*1	•	•		•	41			•		U/K	•					
26. Becky Godden-Edwards	•	•		•	20	P		•		•	•				•	
27. Thi Hai Nguyen*1				•	20			U/K	U/K	U/K	•				•	
28. Claudia Lawrence*1		•		•	35				•	U/K			R Foss via R Ouse	•		
29. Sian O'Callaghan*1*2	•			•	22	•		•		•	•				•	
Deposition Site 1																
Deposition site 2																
Ramsbury Trophy Store																

		Trophies kept		Deposition method							Deposition site				Halliwell's specific knowledge of the deposition sites*			Counter police measures	
Victim was strangled	Victim was stabbed	Items of clothing missing as a "trophy" and/or to prevent forensic analysis	Clothing found in "Trophy Store"	Victim killed in one place, body transported by car to deposition site	Body concealed	Interval between disappearance and discovery in months of the body in months if more than one month	Body deposited in bin bags	Body deposited in carpet	Body found on a canal or riverbank and/or had been deposited in water	Body buried	Knife and /or instruments used to murder, dismember and/or mutilate corpse not found	Deposition site in rural area	Deposition site on or near canal or river bank, or in water	Deposition site in urban area	Deposition site known to Halliwell from residence or work	Deposition site probably known to Halliwell from residence or work	Canals, waterways and fishing places close to the deposition sites Halliwell may have used, or is known to have used	Abduction and deposition sites in different police force areas	Attempt made to destroy or conceal forensic evidence
21	22	23	24	25	26	27	28	29	30	31	32	33	34	35	36	37	38	39	40
		•		•		264+	•							•			Rochdale Canal	?	•
•		•		•		4			•			•			•		Blenheim Lake,Oxford Canal	?	•
	•	•		•		4			•			•			•		Kingston Seymour, Severn Estuary		•
	•			•	•						•					•	Leeds and Liverpool Canal, Pennington Flash	•	•
	•	•		KIS	KIS			KIS	KIS	KIS	KIS	•			KIS	KIS	KIS	R Tees, R Skerne, Middleton St George		•
N/D		•		•	•			•		•		•	•				Leeds & Liverpool Canal, Pennington Flash		•
	•	•		•												•	Saffordshire and Worcestershire Canal, Shropshire Union Canal, R Severn (D), Gillies Pool (D)		•
•		•		•					•		•		•				Sharpness Canal		•
•		•		•						•						•	Ladybower Reservoir, Speedwell Cavern		•
																		?	•
		•		•	•									•		•	R Witham, Grantham Canal		
•		•		•								•			•		Leeds and Liverpool Canal		•
•	N/R			KIS	•	5			•								Rochdale Canal		•
																		?	•
N/D		•		•		52	•		•		•	•	•		•			•	•
																		?	•
?				•	•	1	•				•	•	•				Grand Union Canal	?	•
																		?	•
		•		•	•			•						•		•	Rochdale Canal, River Irwell		•
		•				2					•	•					Scaling Dam	•	•
	•			KIS	KIS			KIS	KIS	KIS	KIS	•			•		Shefield and Tinsley Canal	•	•
																		?	•
•			•		•	97			•		•	•			•			•	•
																		?	•
						?										•	R Foss via R Ouse, University Lake	?	•
•	•	•		•	•					•		•	•		•			•	•
											•	•	•			•	R Leven, Ramsbury		•

Appendix II

Code C PACE 2010 – How It Affected the First Trial

PACE Code C sets out the requirements for the detention, treatment and questioning of suspects. Within this book we have referred to this on a number of occasions, mainly when discussing the ruling that Mrs Justice Cox made that Halliwell's confessions to killing each of the women were inadmissible as evidence. As stated, she said that this was because Detective Superintendent Steve Fulcher had breached the guidelines by failing to caution Halliwell and denying him access to a solicitor during the period that the confessions were obtained. This led to Becky's murder not being brought to trial until years later.

The requirements for how a suspect should be detained, treated and questioned are, of course, incredibly important. They ensure everyone is treated fairly. But the police are faced with a number of legal constraints to work within, and in an unprecedented scenario like the one Steve Fulcher was faced with on the 24 March 2011, the guidelines can become difficult to follow.

In accordance with PACE, Halliwell had already been arrested and cautioned prior to the 'urgent interview'. The caution is as follows: 'You do not have to say anything, but it may harm your defence if you do not mention when questioned something which you later rely on in court. Anything you do say may be given in evidence.'

The possibility of Halliwell confessing to another murder could not have been foreseen. Consequently, Steve Fulcher was unprepared and having to make decisions alone in a complex, developing, life and death situation, without the benefit of advice from senior colleagues. Additionally he had to have reasonable suspicion to arrest Halliwell and caution him for murder (Becky) and under the circumstances we the authors believe that he did not, as there were no other missing women that Wiltshire Police were looking for at that moment in time. Even up to the point when Halliwell took Steve Fulcher to Eastleach there was no conclusion until days later when Becky's remains were recovered.

Steve Fulcher was operating in an extraordinary and unprecedented situation where there is uncertainty about the application of PACE. And after the arrest, the Chief Constable issued a force wide message to say how 'brilliantly' managed the enquiry was: 'I particularly extend my thanks to Detective Superintendent Steve Fulcher for the bold and confident approach to the investigation.' Which indicated that senior officers concurred with his belief that his actions were lawful and compliant with PACE, at the time.

So firstly we will look at how PACE stood in 2011. The following is taken from Policy paper PACE Code C 2008. The requirements for the detention, treatment and questioning of suspects not related to terrorism in police custody. Published 17 May 2010. From: Home Office.

10   Cautions
       (a) When a caution must be given

10.1 A person whom there are grounds to suspect of an offence, see Note 10A, must be cautioned before any questions about an offence, or further questions if the answers provide the grounds for suspicion, are put to them if either the suspect's answers or silence, (i.e., failure or refusal to answer or answer satisfactorily) may be given in evidence to a court in a prosecution.

Christopher Halliwell was cautioned at 11:06am on Thursday 24 March 2011 when arrested in the Asda Car Park and subject to a short urgent interview of eight minutes.

> 11.1 Following a decision to arrest a suspect, they must not be interviewed about the relevant offence except at a police station or other authorised place of detention, unless the consequent delay would be likely to:
>
> (a) lead to:
> - interference with, or harm to, evidence connected with an offence;
> - interference with, or physical harm to, other people; or
> - serious loss of, or damage to, property;
>
> (c) hinder the recovery of property obtained in consequence of the commission of an offence.
>
> Interviewing in any of these circumstances shall cease once the relevant risk has been averted or the necessary questions have been put to attempt to avert that risk.

As we see it, there was indeed still a risk of interference with, or physical harm to, Sian at this point. No one except Christopher Halliwell knew whether or not she was alive. There was also the risk of a loss of or damage to property, Sian's clothing, or items with Halliwell's DNA on. Therefore, our interpretation is that the urgent review could continue, until a time when the police recovered Sian and the relevant forensic evidence.

Next, let's take a look at the other side to the challenge Steve Fulcher faced; The Human Rights Act 1998. As discussed, Steve Fulcher was working on the assumption that Sian was still alive, that this was a kidnapping case, and that he had to find her. Article 2 of the Human

Rights Act protects your right to life, meaning that nobody can try to end your life and that the Government should take appropriate measures to safeguard life by making laws to protect you and, in some circumstances, by taking steps to protect you if your life is at risk.

The law says:

> Article 2 of the Human Rights Act protects your right to life.

This means that nobody, including the Government, can try to end your life. It also means the Government should take appropriate measures to safeguard life by making laws to protect you and, in some circumstances, by taking steps to protect you if your life is at risk.

Public authorities should also consider your right to life when making decisions that might put you in danger or that affect your life expectancy.

If a member of your family dies in circumstances that involve the state, you may have the right to an investigation. The state is also required to investigate suspicious deaths and deaths in custody. The courts have decided that the right to life does not include a right to die.

Are there any restrictions to this right? Article 2 is often referred to as an 'absolute right'. These are rights that can never be interfered with by the state.

1. Everyone's right to life shall be protected by law. No one shall be deprived of his life intentionally.

Therefore, Steve Fulcher had to make a decision, and we believe he made the correct one. In our opinion the victim's right to life should outweigh the suspect's right to silence.

We believe that on balance, Steve Fulcher made the right call. He had already arrested and cautioned Halliwell prior to the 'urgent interview' and Halliwell was not a vulnerable person and understood the arrest process from previous convictions. The IPCC investigation found that 'Mr Godden's complaint that Det Supt Fulcher's actions led to the murder charge in respect of Rebecca being dropped is upheld.' It is now clear that the charge was dropped because of a ruling on admissibility of evidence that was in error and because the CPS did not challenge the ruling at the time. This is a failure of the legal system, not of Steve Fulcher.

The IPCC investigation states that 'Det Supt Fulcher stated had he not proceeded as he did, Rebecca's remains may never have been found. However, it is not possible to determine what may or may not have happened if Mr Halliwell had been immediately conveyed to custody after his arrest and urgent interview by detectives'. This is true. But there is no doubt that Fulcher's actions resulted in the recovery of the body and the subsequent conviction. Whilst the possibility of Halliwell suddenly confessing to a murder, having been advised by a solicitor not to, appears to us to be remote.

The IPCC report states that Fulcher's reasons for breaching PACE were 'not relevant for the purposes of the investigation'. Given that His Honour Sir John Griffith Williams later upheld them, at Halliwell's second trial, we believe that this shows they clearly were relevant.

We also feel that Steve Fulcher was treated unfairly by Wiltshire Police. His misconduct hearing was held privately, Wiltshire Police excluded the public from the hearing and held it 'in camera' or in private. This is now prohibited, although we do not know when this change was put into place, to ensure that the system is 'accountable and transparent', and whilst one of the charges against Steve Fulcher was dropped at the start of the misconduct hearing, he had nonetheless had the stress of preparing to face a charge. He was faced with three charges at this misconduct hearing, although the second was dropped, and Wiltshire Police tried to introduce a fourth charge that he had been dishonest towards the end of the hearing without any warning but the panel properly unanimously refused to hear it.

The first charge brought against him was Charge 1, 'The failure of Fulcher to adhere to PACE including that he obtained a confession from Halliwell by oppression.' But the later ruling of His Honour Sir John Griffith Williams that Fulcher was not oppressive or responsible for the charge of murdering Miss Godden-Edwards being dropped goes against this entirely. Although he could not have access to the Operation Mayan Gold Policy File, recording senior officer approval for all the decisions he took during Operation Mayan, Fulcher obtained a copy of a recommendation he received in 2011 for the QPM from a whistle-blower within Wiltshire Police:

> There is no doubt that without his direct intervention and engagement with the suspect, the bodies of both young women would not have been located'. …This is but a flavour of his remarkable and sustained contribution' …. [He is] 'a man of integrity, whose achievements not only enhanced the reputation of Wiltshire Police but upheld and demonstrated the best traditions of British Policing.

This evidence demonstrated that Fulcher's actions were believed to be appropriate and approved of by senior officers of Wiltshire Police at the time.

Charge 2, 'Fulcher had released information to the media alleged to be prejudicial to Halliwell's right to a fair trial after Halliwell's arrest.' was dropped. In his book, Steve Fulcher suggests that the reason Charge 2 was dropped at the start of the hearing was that Fulcher's actions were approved by a team of senior officers in the Operation Mayan Gold Group; his actions included the media strategy, which in his opinion makes them complicit. After extensive cross examination and hearing legal argument, Her Honour Mrs Justice Cox had already found in court that Fulcher's media strategy constituted 'a serious error of judgment', but he was not acting in bad faith.

Charge 3, 'Unauthorised contact with journalists', referred to an accusation of breaching a judicial order. It was only at the hearing that Wiltshire Police admitted that it had misunderstood the judicial order and that in fact no judicial order had been made to prevent the police speaking to journalists.

There have been calls for reform and clarification of PACE. Swindon's local MP Mr Robin Buckland QC questioned the Prime Minister on the case on 21 November 2012.

He said:

> The person responsible for the murder of Becky Godden-Edwards, whose mother is my constituent, has not been brought to justice because important incriminating evidence was excluded from the court process. Will my right honourable Friend join our cause in calling for a thorough review of code C of the Police and Criminal Evidence Act 1984, so that such terrible situations will not occur in future?

Quoted in the *Evening Standard*, Mr Buckland said:

> But putting myself into his shoes for a moment, putting aside my legal hat having been a criminal barrister for twenty years, I can entirely understand that in the heat of the moment, when it was still thought that Sian O'Callaghan may still be alive, that that officer thought he was acting in the best interests of the safety of Sian and in the interests of finding out more from Halliwell. The codes of practice are not tablets of stone, they are regularly updated in the light of experience…it is now time that we had another look.

We are concerned that PACE has still not been reviewed or updated. Whilst the situation Steve Fulcher found himself in with Christopher Halliwell was totally unprecedented, it could of course happen again. Another senior investigating officer could well find themselves in this difficult position of choosing between their career or making a decision that ultimately finds a missing person.

Appendix III

Support

We would like to highlight some resources available to you that you can contact if you are a victim of crime or if you have been affected by the cases discussed in this book.

Victim Support

Victim Support is an independent charity dedicated to supporting victims of crime and traumatic incidents in England and Wales. They provide specialist help to support people to cope and recover to the point where they feel they are back on track with their lives.

They say:

> Need help after crime?
> Independent. Free. Confidential.
>
> Fill in our online form for support and advice. Someone from your local victim care team will contact you within three working days (Mon to Fri). If you want to speak to someone now, call our free 24/7 Support Line on 08 08 16 89 111 or start a live chat. In an emergency always call 999.
>
> Our service is confidential and we will only share information about you without your consent if we're

worried about your safety or someone else's safety, or if we are required to by law.

There are lots of different types of crime, and people will react to crime differently. If you've been affected by crime and need support or information, please contact us.

National Ugly Mugs (NUM) - Ending Violence Against Sex Workers

National Ugly Mugs (NUM) is a pioneering, national organisation which provides greater access to justice and protection for sex workers who are often targeted by dangerous individuals but are frequently reluctant to report these incidents to the police. These offenders are often serial sexual predators who pose a huge risk to the public as a whole.

They say:

> Ugly Mugs schemes were first introduced in Victoria, Australia in 1986 by the Prostitutes Collective, they realised that circulating descriptions of 'ugly mugs' could warn other sex workers about dangerous people and situations.

Our Mission: Ending Violence Against Sex Workers

Our values: We believe in and advocate for the human rights of sex workers including;

- the right to self determination
- the right to live free from violence
- the right to live free from intimidation, coercion or exploitation
- the right to work as safely as possible
- the right to police protection

What we do: We take reports of incidents from sex workers and produce anonymised warnings which are sent directly to sex workers and front-line support projects throughout the UK. With consent, we share anonymous intelligence to the police. We support sex workers in making full reports to the police so that the perpetrators can be identified, arrested and convicted. We ensure sex workers have access to professional services when they have been a victim of crime.

Our Aims:

- To improve the safety of sex workers
- To prevent crime
- To bring to justice more offenders who target sex workers.
- To support sex workers in accessing frontline services
- To increase the number of crimes against sex workers reported to the police
- To enhance the levels of intelligence that exist throughout the UK about dangerous criminals

There are various reasons for ugly mugs schemes, sex workers in some sectors frequently suffer violence and other crimes committed by people presenting as clients, also sex workers are also often reluctant to make formal complaints to the police and so records do not reflect actual prevalence of how common this violence can be. However, offenders need to be identified because they may attack other sex workers, with studies showing men who murder sex workers frequently have a history of violence against sex workers and others.

About the Authors

Chris Clark

Chris is a retired police intelligence officer and true crime author.

During 2011 when Christopher Halliwell was arrested for the double murders of Becky Godden-Edwards and Sian O'Callaghan both from Swindon, I was heavily into writing my late father's RAF biography which was published in 2012, also a further RAF WW2 spin-off book which I had self-published and research into Robert Black, the serial child killer for a later 2017 book, *The Face Of Evil* co-authored with Robert Giles and published by John Blake.

Just the year before my wife Jeanne had told me of an incident which occurred to her during the early 1970's which bore all the hallmarks of an attempted abduction by Robert Black. Thus I was far too busy to pay the Halliwell case much attention.

The same applied during October 2012 when Halliwell was convicted at Bristol Crown Court of the murder of Sian O'Callaghan, but Becky Godden-Edwards case not proceeded with. At this time I was researching unsolved murders of unaccompanied females which had occurred mainly in England throughout the 1970's. This led to a 2015 book *Yorkshire Ripper: The Secret Murders* co-authored by Tim Tate and published by John Blake.

The first time that I started researching murders that I felt were attributable to Christopher Halliwell was during June 2014 when there was a press release that police had discovered a 'secret lair' of convicted murderer Christopher Halliwell during searches of land surrounding a pond in Ramsbury, Wiltshire. Searches of the area near Hilldrop Lane, which started on May 14, came to an end. It followed the discovery of a one of a pair of boots which belonged to 2011 murder victim Sian O'Callaghan, and a single barrelled shotgun in a pond in the village.

In the following days, fingertip searches by police, including with the use of cadaver dogs trained in tracing human remains, were carried out, and the pond was drained to allow specialist teams to search its bed. A pile of material said to consist of around sixty pieces, some of which are believed to be women's clothing, were found buried around one hundred yards from the site and a chunky knit cardigan was also found close to the pond. All items had been sent for forensic examination. The cardigan was subsequently identified as having belonged to Becky Godden-Edwards.

From that moment on I became intensely interested in Christopher Halliwell, as the inference in the media was that there could be a further substantial number of unsolved reported female murders and unknown murdered missing women that he had not been held to account for.

I knew from police press statements that during the years from 1987 to when he was arrested in 2011 that he had held numerous jobs as a ground worker and taxi driver all over the United Kingdom as well as owning an incredible number of eighty motor vehicles in those twenty-four years, averaging three a year. I also knew that he engaged in visiting popular narrowboat venues and was a keen fisherman.

This is when me, Bethan and others began to methodically research Halliwell and the other crimes we felt he was responsible for.

By August 2014 there were a number of cases I felt should be drawn to the attention of the police, the 1983 murder of Eila Karjalainen, mother-of-two Shelley Morgan, Lindsay Jo Rimer and Julie Findley. An article linking Eila, Shelley Morgan and Lindsay Jo's cases were published in a national newspaper and as a result I was contacted by a detective from the joint Brunel Avon & Somerset/Wiltshire Major Investigation Team who subsequently interviewed me about my knowledge of the cases and why I thought they should consider Christopher Halliwell as a suspect. At this time, I also sent an e-mail to Merseyside Police, explaining my reasons for believing Halliwell as a viable suspect in their investigations into Julie Finley's murder.

I have not heard from either force on Julie's case since.

In the meantime, my research put into double figures the number of cases which seemed to fit with the method of Christopher Halliwell. My ever-growing list of cases included a significant number where the offender had abducted the victim from one police force area to a bordering one. This was evident in both murders Halliwell had been convicted for; Sian O'Callaghan was abducted from Swindon in Wiltshire, firstly taken to Savernake Forest and the borders of Berkshire before finally being dumped in south Oxfordshire, and Becky Godden-Edwards had been abducted from Swindon and buried in a field in south Gloucestershire.

I also identified a *'cluster'* of cases in a triangular area comprising Liverpool, Wigan and Manchester known as *'The East Lancs Ripper'* series, where the victim had been both abducted from near a popular waterway and dumped in a similar area. This *modus operandi* was indicative to me of Halliwell's involvement, knowing that Halliwell had previously resided and worked in the Liverpool area, coupled with the popular narrowboat and fishing areas where these victims' remains had been dumped.

By the end of September 2016 when Halliwell was finally convicted of Becky Godden-Edwards 2003 murder I had amassed sufficient research to be able to pass on my findings to the detective who had visited me some two years previously. He said that he would submit an intelligence report to his supervisors working on the joint Wiltshire/Avon and Somerset investigation. Details of these cases was also published in a national newspaper in order to draw public attention to Halliwell in the hope that it might produce some *'sightings'* of him over the years in these areas.

At the end of 2016 I contacted former Detective Superintendent Steve Fulcher by e-mail and passed on to him my list of potential victims of Christopher Halliwell. He got back to me in June 2017 and confirmed he felt the MO details of the cases submitted were consistent with the known facts attributable to Halliwell. He referred to the clothing found at Hilldrop, saying: 'They have a significant problem in their failure to examine the trophy store. Your research should provide them with pointers as to whom these items belong. Should an evidential link be found, we would be well on the way to clearing up these cases'.

During the middle of January 2017 Ben Wilkinson of 'The Mail On Sunday' took up the gauntlet and sent me an e-mail to let me know that he had contacted the Halliwell Investigation Team, but he confirmed that whilst Wiltshire Police did get back to him saying one of the victims on the list was being looked at, they didn't want to say any more. It was his impression that they are reluctant to keep unnecessarily dragging up cold cases in the press so avoid upsetting the families, but he told me that he would keep checking in with them and let me know whether he got any news.

We identified a further three women who had been abducted from the centre of Middlesbrough, and these were also loosely linked together by Cleveland Police when they announced to the press in April 2018: 'Cleveland Police is setting up a new department to re-investigate the murders of three women on Teesside. The families of Donna Keogh, Vicky Glass and Rachel Wilson have faced years of agony after their loved ones went missing.' Assistant chief constable Jason Harwin said: 'There is commonality between the cases through the sex and ages of the victims and all being linked geographically to Middlesbrough. It is too early in the re-investigations to say if there are any other links.'

During June 2018 we utilised a contact page for Cleveland Police and I passed on my thoughts concerning Halliwell as a suspect for these murders. A detective from Cleveland MT contacted me and said that at some stage officers would visit and view my research on him. He did say that they had started looking at Halliwell and would value my research so far, but that there may be a delay on this. I asked them to obtain Halliwell's known timeline for north-east from Wilts and to check the clothing against their victims. As we have discussed on a number of occasions throughout this book, Cleveland Police have not been back in touch with me despite a promising start; quite often we have found our questions left unanswered or requests refused.

In the ten years since Christopher Halliwell's arrest for the double murders not one police force has announced any further investigation into his involvement in any unsolved crimes. No further victims have been identified the police in the ten years following Christopher Halliwell's arrest and taking him out of circulation. We believe this needs to be assessed from a central point, that being the National Crime Agency.

Within the content of this book I and my co-author Bethan Trueman have set out our research and investigation of other murders we feel the various police forces should look at in depth for linkage to Christopher Halliwell. Only time will tell if we are on the right track.

The aim of this book is for the authors to assess the other unsolved victims of Christopher Halliwell and point the various police forces involved in that direction. Our mission is for truth and justice for the victims and some closure for the families left behind.

Bethan Trueman

I am a mother of two living in Swindon with my husband and our families. Alongside my day job I am also one half of the podcast *Seeing Red*, which began in 2018. This is a podcast where myself and my friend and co-host Mark discuss true crime cases, releasing an episode each week. I have always been fascinated by the darker side to humanity, and the quest for justice when it comes to evil people.

Chris Clark approached me to write this book with him because of my links to writing about true crime and especially cases from the UK. I was aware of Chris from his other books in which I knew he had worked tirelessly to ensure stories were shared and victims' names were not forgotten, and so I knew this would be the right person to collaborate with. He wanted to work together to look at women potentially murdered by Halliwell, and to bring these names to the forefront of people's minds, as well as to prompt the police to look into these cases further. Being from Wiltshire and having ties to Christopher Halliwell's local area meant I really felt that I had a responsibility to help bring these stories into the open.

Former Detective Superintendent Steve Fulcher says, in his book *Catching a Serial Killer*, that he was surprised to realise Swindon was not, as he first assumed, an anonymous commuter town devoid of community spirit. It is a place that is often used as the butt of a joke, but for the people who make their home here it is a great place to live and bring up families. People tend to know their neighbours, and plenty of community events take place, even though it is geographically and population-wise large for a town. And when a tragedy happens in a small close-knit community it sends shockwaves that are felt for years.

I, like many others in the local area, had a couple of loose connections to Sian O'Callaghan. Sian's disappearance and the subsequent realisation that she had been murdered was shocking to us all. I was just nineteen years old, trying to reassure a work friend their sister would surely be home safe soon, whilst also reminding my own sisters and my friends to be vigilant. It later transpired that I had some connections to Halliwell too, like many others, and again this is not unusual in a small town; this just added to the pain felt by the community. This was a man who had babysat for a family member, who had been a drinking buddy of one of my loved ones. This was a man who had been trusted by many to get them home safe and was well known in the community. But we were now finding out about this dark side to him that hadn't been suspected before.

As the years passed, we learned even more about Christopher Halliwell. His hiding place at the pond near Ramsbury was discovered and subsequently drained, revealing potential trophies from over fifty potential victims. And Halliwell was finally convicted of Becky's murder, a young woman whose mother had campaigned locally and nationally for justice for many years. But it is never far from my mind about whether he was responsible for the deaths of many other women.

Some of the names Chris brought to me were names I knew already, cases I had looked into before, women I had discussed with friends, women whose murders or disappearances I had read about and watched documentaries about over the years. A number of the names were not familiar to me, but through my research and from writing about them, I now know those names and those stories so well.

I feel strongly that these cases simply must be investigated further, that there are links here that cannot and should not be ignored. I hope that Wiltshire Police and the other forces across the UK will decide to look into Christopher Halliwell's potential as a serial killer, and whilst it will have taken a long time it could mean finally getting answers for so many people. My dream is that we can prompt police forces to look at these cases in more detail going forward.

Writing this book has not been easy; after spending time writing each day I hug my family that little bit closer, feeling real pain for the women and for their families who have not been able to get justice. I hope that this book may help the families of the women discussed here, knowing their loved ones are not and will not be forgotten.

Acknowledgements

Three people we have singled out to thank, who have been actively instrumental in contributing and producing articles on Christopher Halliwell's other potentially unsolved murders, are Andrew Gardner, Tim Hicks and Scott Williams-Collier.

Andrew Gardner is a former Crime Correspondent at the Sunday Mirror and is now Freelance; he regularly contributes to the Daily Star Sunday and co-writes in other nationals. He has worked on some of the biggest national and international crime stories of the last two decades, including the murder of TV star Jill Dando, the Soham murders, the killing of Rachel Nickell on Wimbledon Common, 9/11 and 7/7 in the UK and the continuing investigation into the crimes of Christopher Halliwell. As a freelance journalist since 2006, he has worked closely with Chris Clark to expose the links between known killers, rapists and paedophiles to many unsolved cold case murders. He has been since 2014 working with, and continues to work with, Chris, on a number of articles that keeps Christopher Halliwell as a serial killer in the national public eye.

Tim Hicks is a Chartered Accountant and Journalist, he contributes regular co-authored feature articles with Chris in the NYE (North Yorks Enquirer) covering a complete analysis of Christopher Halliwell and his potential unsolved victims and challenging various forces with our uncovered evidence, trying to where possible to have unsolved cases aired with Christopher Halliwell as the prime facia suspect.

Scott Williams-Collier is an avid true crime buff who has been invaluable in airing the *'East Lancs Ripper'* series in his podcast, as well as interviewing Chris on his show. Chris' work highlighting Halliwell as a viable suspect meant he had a witness come forward who has tied Halliwell to the area, confirming he lived in nearby Aughton. His hope is that one day these cases will finally be solved, and justice will prevail for these young ladies who lost their lives in the most brutal way imaginable.

We thank all three for their continuing and tireless contributions.

We would also like to refer you to the following books which have been incredibly useful to us in our research.

A Killer's Confession: How I Brought My Daughter's Murderer to Justice

By Karen Edwards

Catching a Serial Killer: My hunt for murderer Christopher Halliwell
By Stephen Fulcher

Karen's book has given us a real insight into Becky, her childhood and upbringing but sadly the difficulties she faced, as well as her murder and the events surrounding the discovery of her body and the subsequent trial. This book highlighted the hard work Karen did through her campaigns for justice and that she continues to undertake.

Steve's was vital in helping us to understand the struggles he faced in getting justice for these two women, even at the cost of his career, as well as the investigative work the police undertook in their hunt. His support to us with this book and his help in answering the many questions we have posed to him has been invaluable.

Index